CHANGE, LEAD, SUCCEED

Building Capacity With School Leadership Teams

Linda Munger

and Valerie von Frank

National Staff Development Council
www.nsdc.org

National Staff Development Council
504 S. Locust St.
Oxford, OH 45056
513-523-6029
800-727-7288
Fax: 513-523-0638
E-mail: NSDCoffice@nsdc.org
www.nsdc.org

Change, Lead, Succeed:
Building Capacity With School Leadership Teams
By Linda Munger and Valerie von Frank

Editor: Valerie von Frank
Copy editor: Sue Chevalier
Designers: Stacey Sanders, Cheryl Addington, Sue Chevalier
Cover design: Kitty Black

Printed in the United States of America
Item #B468

ISBN 978-0-9800393-8-2

Contents

Tools on the CD

Acknowledgments

Often when I arrived home after working with educators or finishing a lengthy evaluation report on professional development, my husband, Jim, reminded me of the importance of writing a book about what I was learning as a result of my work. As I worked with schools and districts across the country, educators would ask me if I had ever written a book and, if not, why not. Thus, after much encouragement, I began my journey writing about the role of a leadership team in leading school change.

I could not have done this without the love and constant support of my husband and my two sons, Bob and Dan, who have always been there to assist me in my efforts to make a difference for students and educators. I am thankful to my dear friends, colleagues, and clients who have helped me on this journey of writing, whether it was giving me the opportunity to work and learn with them, stretching my thinking about how to lead changes in professional learning at the school level, giving me ideas on how best to help leadership teams, or reviewing chapters during the early stages of writing this book.

As a senior consultant for NSDC, I have had access to and been able to use in the field with great success many of the organization's published materials. NSDC has granted readers access to a host of wonderful tools on the CD that accompanies this book. I am grateful for the opportunity to work with and learn from NSDC Deputy Executive Director Joellen Killion, who has constantly encouraged me in writing this book. Words cannot express enough my gratitude to the editor, Valerie von Frank, who has helped me from the very beginning in getting a coherent outline, giving me feedback and encouragement, and performing awesome editing in order to finish this project. I also am thankful for the superb attention to detail provided by copy editor Sue Chevalier, who ensured the text was as flawless as possible and assembled the tools on the CD. I am indebted to Kitty Black for her dynamic cover art and to Stacey Sanders and Cheryl Addington for their expertise in designing the inside of the book to draw the reader's attention to key material.

In sum, I am grateful for all the educators who have enriched my life through numerous learning experiences of changing, leading, and being successful in making a difference in the lives of students and educators. Most of all, to my family, thank you for helping me reach my goal of writing my first book.

— *Linda Munger*

Foreword

Change, Lead, Succeed: Building Capacity With School Leadership Teams is a tool kit for school leadership teams and school or district professional development committees. The information and resources are all here to help teams accomplish their work of planning, implementing, monitoring, and evaluating effective professional learning necessary to achieve the school's goals for student achievement. The book is rich with easy-to-access tools for teams at the earliest stages of development and for those who have been doing this work for years but want to refine their practice to have a greater impact on educators and their students.

School leadership teams can easily get caught up in addressing virtually every issue, problem, challenge, or whim that emerges. *Change, Lead, Succeed* makes it clear that a school leadership team's primary function is professional learning, work that doesn't leave space for those distracting tasks that often derail the team from its core mission. Underlying the text is the assumption that when adults in a school are learning together and collaborating about how to implement what they are learning, trust, innovation, and relationships grow. When the learning is tied to the content standards and students are expected to focus on essential areas for improvement identified in a wide variety of data sources and master them, results soar.

A book by an educator as experienced as Linda Munger has enormous potential to help school leadership teams actively shape their pathway to becoming collaborative communities committed to student achievement. Munger has spent decades as a skillful and respected educational consultant. She has amassed tremendous wisdom not only from extensive reading and informal and formal learning, but from visiting schools, listening to teachers and principals, coaching them, and consulting with them as they grapple with their most significant challenges related to student learning. She brings this knowledge gained from schools and districts in California, Iowa, Wisconsin, Pennsylvania, and Indiana, among others, to readers she otherwise might not encounter.

Valerie von Frank is NSDC's book editor and an education writer whose wealth of knowledge about professional learning has led to numerous articles for *JSD* and other NSDC publications. Her research and analytical skills are also evident in these pages. She brings to this work her extensive experience with NSDC resources, publications, and tools, as well as her ability to conceptualize what will be most useful to practitioners in accomplishing their work.

Not every school leadership team has the opportunity to meet face-to-face in conference rooms or classrooms with facilitators such as Munger who will stretch team members' thinking. This book substitutes for the collaborative conversations she would have facilitated. Dedicated teacher leaders and school principals can use it to initiate and extend those conversations as if she were present as a partner.

I have had opportunities to learn from Munger's experiences, listen to her challenges, and problem solve with her as she worked with numerous schools and districts, and I am particularly honored to write the foreword to this book. Readers will want to dive into this resource with sticky notes and highlighters ready. Few copies will remain pristine for more than a few minutes.

— *Joellen Killion*
Deputy executive director
National Staff Development Council

Introduction

The purpose of this book is to redefine the role of school leadership teams. To lead continuous improvement, administrators and teacher leaders need to be catalysts for change. They need new skills and knowledge — of collaboration, change processes, high-quality professional development, evaluation, and more — to help colleagues adapt instruction to students' needs so every child achieves at high levels.

As site-based leaders of change, school leadership team members ensure that all educators experience high-quality professional learning so that all students experience quality teaching. Team members plan ways for teachers to examine their current practices and identify the knowledge and skills they need to improve.

To lead this new approach of continuous improvement, the National Staff Development Council has redefined professional development as a process in which educators engage in "a cycle in which they analyze data, determine student and adult learning goals based on that analysis, design joint lessons that use evidence-based strategies, have access to coaches for support in improving their classroom instruction, and then assess how their learning and teamwork affects student achievement" (Hirsh, 2009).

This book will help administrators and teacher leaders understand the cycle and find new ways to lead the charge for continuous improvement through a collaborative team effort at the school level.

HOW TO USE THIS BOOK

This book is meant to help principals and teacher leaders develop their own capacity to lead continuous improvement of the faculty's instructional practice, leading to improved student performance.

Each chapter will help members of the school leadership team develop their knowledge and understanding of leadership behaviors to successfully plan, implement, and evaluate high-quality professional learning for continuous instructional improvement that increases student performance.

Use Chapter 1, *Defining the Leadership Team,* to learn what distinguishes a school leadership team from other school teams, clarify the school leadership team's role in building school capacity through job-embedded, school-centered professional learning, and identify a process for selecting school leadership team members.

Chapter 2, *Learning to Lead,* outlines essential knowledge team members need. Delve into four areas of understanding for team members: members' roles and responsibilities, a definition of high-quality professional development, change as a process, and the basics of teamwork.

In Chapter 3, *Planning School-Based Professional Learning,* examine the skills and practices for leading school-based professional learning. Begin by analyzing student achievement data at the building level to determine student and teacher needs, use data to develop a professional development plan as part of the school improvement plan, and incorporate NSDC's Standards for Staff Development into the design of a professional development program. Examine six characteristics of professional learning that correlate with positive changes in teacher knowledge and skills, and find how to engage in and facilitate different forms of professional learning.

The purpose of Chapter 4, *Supporting School-Based Professional Learning,* is to help readers design structures that engage teachers in ongoing professional learning at the school level, model strategies/protocols for skill development and continuous improvement, demonstrate and provide feedback during the transfer of learning, and organize and/or facilitate collaborative coaching experiences for all educators at the school level.

Chapter 5, *Evaluating the Impact,* provides examples of how to monitor and evaluate the effect of professional learning on improving instructional practices to raise student achievement.

Finally, follow and use a case study presented in Chapter 6 as a model for your own team.

Each of the first five chapters offers background information to build knowledge and understanding, suggests ideas of where to begin the work needed to build the leadership team, offers ideas for additional resources team members can study and use in their work together or with teachers, and provides tools to get started. The information is presented not as a linear progression. Some groups may find they need only portions of a chapter or may skip pieces altogether before cycling back. The chapters outline the work of the leadership team and, along with the resource list in each, are starting points for the group as it forms and works to create and sustain school change.

"Leadership as we have attempted it has not usually mobilized staff to adapt their practices and beliefs to emerging student and societal needs. … It takes a 'community of leaders' (Barth, 2001) to truly mobilize a school so that teaching and learning change and improve."

— Gordon A. Donaldson Jr., *Cultivating Leadership in Schools: Connecting People, Purpose, and Practice*, 2006

Chapter 1

DEFINING
the leadership team

THE CASE FOR LEADERSHIP

Leadership is the catalyst that can bring about school improvement. That case has been made in literature and research. But the fundamental notion of school leadership continues to change, from a redefinition of the principal's role over the last several decades through iterations of distributed leadership or stewardship.

Studies have found leadership has an effect on student achievement second only to the impact of quality teaching (Leithwood, Aitken, & Jantzi, 2006; Silins & Mulford, 2002; Mortimore, Sammons, Stoll, Lewis, & Ecob, 1988). With economic, social, and political globalization affecting public education in the United States, schools have been called upon to raise standards. For schools to meet

the challenges of a new age, to be able to help every child achieve academically and graduate prepared to lead a productive life, strong leadership is essential.

Societal changes have created "adaptive challenges," the term used by leadership researchers Ronald Heifetz and Donald Laurie (1997) to describe issues an organization faces that require it to change its practices at a deep level to be able to survive. Heifetz and Laurie say adaptive challenges "are often systemic problems with no ready answers" (p. 124). As policy makers have pressured schools for greater accountability and improved student performance among a wider range of children in response to societal change, schools are struggling to find new ways to operate in a changed environment. This new environment challenges deeply held beliefs, questions values that were accepted in the past, and poses "legitimate yet competing perspectives" (Heifetz & Laurie, 1997, p. 124).

The definition of leadership over the last several decades has changed. Principals have been called on to shift from a management role to one of leading instructional change. Researchers have stressed instructional leadership since at least the 1980s (Brookover & Lezotte, 1982; Duke, 1982; Levine & Lezotte, 1990; Kroeze, 1984).

Lawrence Lezotte writes (in Miller & Vruggink, 1983), "In the effective schools, the teachers recognize the need for coordination and support. They look to and expect their principals to be instructional leaders. In turn, principals feel a sense of responsibility to discharge the leadership role. As a result, the principals are much closer to the day-to-day instructional program, closely monitor pupil progress, and provide systematic feedback on goal attainment throughout the school year."

Stronge (1988) writes, "If principals are to heed the call from educational reformers to become instructional leaders, it is obvious that they must take on a dramatically different role" (p. 33). Michael Fullan (1991) found in his research that "schools operated by principals who were perceived by their teachers to be strong instructional leaders exhibited significantly greater gain scores in achievement in reading and mathematics than did schools operated by average and weak instructional leaders" (p. 156).

Rick DuFour (2002) parses the definition of instructional leader by shifting the focus for the principal from teachers to student learning, adding: "I had focused on the questions, 'What are the teachers teaching?' and 'How can I help them to teach it more effectively?' Instead, my efforts should have been driven by the questions, 'To what extent are the students learning the intended outcomes of each course?' and 'What

The team's role

To fulfill the role of the school leadership team, Stephanie Hirsh (2007) indicates that members are responsible for and receive professional development and support to lead by learning to:

- **Adopt school goals** and select appropriate strategies to achieve them;

- **Understand data** related to student performance in order to determine school needs and translate them into goals;

- **Monitor implementation** of school action plans and progress toward achieving school goals;

- **Establish the organization and focus** of specialized learning teams — teams that are issue-driven as opposed to grade-level or course-focused;

- **Recommend priorities** for structuring and scheduling learning teams;

- **Keep staff focused** on essential aspects of improving student performance; and

- **Evaluate opportunities** presented to schools under pressure to improve and limit the number of initiatives allowed (p. 4).

steps can I take to give both students and teachers the additional time and support they need to improve learning?' "

Principals, in addition to the daily requirements of managing staff and a small organization, then added to their responsibilities the challenges of considering ways to improve both student and staff learning.

A report for the Organisation for Economic Co-operation and Development on education leadership in countries around the world notes, "Providing intellectual stimulation, supplying professional development and other support, developing a vision of and focus on learning with others, creating a strong professional learning community through team commitment to learning and achievement — these are the key ways that leaders have exerted their effects on learning, achievement, and performance among students" (Pont, Nusche, & Hopkins, 2008, p. 71).

Recognition is growing that the principal's role in leading schools has become too monumental to be taken on alone. As Donaldson states, "The principal is one player in the leadership mix; how he or she blends in that mix to cultivate leadership throughout will determine his or her contribution to moving the school forward" (2006, p. 4).

Although the principal is the school's instructional leader, the principal can't singlehandedly provide the school leadership needed to engage all staff in a cycle of continuous improvement of teaching and student learning.

"Different leadership will require a transformation of our conception of administration," writes Joseph Murphy (1992, p. 124). "Leaders and leadership in the postindustrial age must look radically different from what they have looked like in the past."

Richard Elmore (2000) says leadership within the school needs to be shared. The idea of distributed leadership is now fairly prevalent in the literature. Research shows that schools with strong, collaborative leadership are the most successful in supporting student achievement. Research by Robert Marzano (2003) on specific school, teacher, and student practices and by Marzano, Timothy Waters, and Brian McNulty (2005) on leadership practices indicates collaborative leadership practices are associated with high levels of student achievement.

"(If) we want better schools, we are going to have to manage and lead differently," Thomas Sergiovanni says succinctly (1992, p. x).

The past focus has been on individual, positional leadership. While a sole leader can help forge the essential vision and create the

> "Different leadership will require a transformation of our conception of administration," writes Joseph Murphy (1992, p. 124). "Leaders and leadership in the postindustrial age must look radically different from what they have looked like in the past."

impetus for improvement, the sole leader is no longer enough. Current research emphasizes a team approach with multiple opportunities for leadership (Lambert, 2003; Fullan, 2004; Kouzes & Posner, 2008) to sustain improvement. Shared leadership leverages educators' capacity for change. Distribution of school leadership acts as a lever for instructional improvement (Camburn & Han, 2008).

Elmore (2000) states, "Distributed

leadership poses the challenge of how to distribute responsibility and authority for guidance and direction of instruction, and learning about instruction, so as to increase the likelihood that the decisions of individual teachers and principals about what to do, and what to learn how to do, aggregate into collective benefits for student learning" (p. 18). Elmore says that distributed leadership, although challenging, is vital to improving instructional practices to impact student learning.

Recognizing that the principal cannot alone

> Leaders of school transformation...inspire, motivate, and support their colleagues through professional learning that leads to improvements in student achievement.

lead the kinds of changes needed to improve achievement for all students, and understanding the challenges of distributing leadership, educators need a model for leadership that accounts for this research.

As researchers demonstrated, sustained improvement hinges on this broader definition of leadership than has existed in the past. High-achieving schools will have an effective principal acting in concert with an effective group of teacher leaders who build the capacity of all within the school to improve student achievement. These teachers will work together not simply as goal-setters, but in school leadership teams.

DEFINING A LEADERSHIP TEAM

The concept of school-based teams clearly is not new. But changes in understanding of

leadership and increased demands on educators, particularly school principals, have created the need for a different kind of leadership.

School leadership teams are different from other school-based teams. Schools have had schoolwide instructional leadership teams, principals' advisory councils, lead teacher committees, and school improvement teams, among other groups. Across states and sometimes within the same district, even the title and work of these teams vary, however, along with how members are selected for the team.

School leadership teams are based on the understanding that change is needed, change must occur at the school level, and school leaders create understanding of change and a sense of urgency and purpose for it. Leadership for change is distributed among multiple people within the school, including the principal, teacher leaders, and perhaps other stakeholders.

School improvement teams support continuous improvement of student achievement. The improvement team's role is different from that of the leadership team, however. The school improvement team has planned overall improvement, lately focused on the expectations for Adequate Yearly Progress as defined by the No Child Left Behind Act. The act of planning is the group's function, although subcommittees in some cases may monitor some specifics.

Other groups focus on aspects of the school's overall improvement plan, such as the student services team or the Response to Intervention team, which target a particular strategy.

The school leadership team, on the other hand, is responsible for planning, implementing, monitoring, and evaluating professional learning in response to student learning needs that the team has worked with staff to identify.

A school leadership team is "a collection of people focused solely on supporting the improvement of student achievement at their school" (McKeever, 2003, p. 4). School leadership teams, Bill McKeever states, "build the capacity of the school staff to participate in a continuous improvement planning process. The focus of this process is on student achievement and creating cultural norms in a school to support it." McKeever calls members of these teams "stewards and monitors of quality implementation of the instructional strategies and programs" who are chosen to improve student learning (p. 4).

The fundamental purpose of the school leadership team is to determine the school's professional learning plan and identify the goals, priorities, and strategies to help implement that plan. The school leadership team must be the central coordinating team in the school. The leadership team ensures that other learning teams' and committees' work is coordinated, and acts as a communication hub for enacting common school goals. Once a school leadership team is formed, the principal and leadership team may decide to review other, existing committees' responsibilities. Some committees may be eliminated. Others may act as subcommittees of the leadership team.

While school leadership teams have been discussed in education literature since the 1990s, they rarely are used in a meaningful form. Schools sometimes have had groups of teacher leaders who decided on matters such as where 4th graders should go on a field trip, whether to have a winter party, or who would collect the book fair money. Other groups have taken responsibility for planning workshops, for example, for school-based training days.

Leaders of school transformation, on the other hand, inspire, motivate, and support their colleagues through professional learning that leads to improvements in student achievement. The focus of their work is continuous improvement of instruction. Such high-performing teams exist in real learning organizations where colleagues support one another in learning, risk taking, innovation, and change (Senge, 1990).

Criteria for selecting teachers to serve on a team

McKeever (2003, p. 52) identified criteria to use in selecting teachers to serve on the leadership team. Criteria include the teacher's:

- **Respect** for and influence among his or her colleagues;

- **Knowledge** and leadership capacity;

- Unique or specialized **perspective** that he or she would bring to the team;

- Grade-level or content area **expertise**;

- Specialized **training** (e.g. special education, reading, English language development);

- **Relationships** with key members of the staff;

- Sense of the **history,** traditions, and context of the school;

- **Aspiration** to become an administrator; and

- Ability to lend **balance** to the makeup of the team.

NSDC's Standards for Staff Development

The National Staff Development Council's Standards for Staff Development are divided among context, process, and content standards.

CONTEXT STANDARDS

Context standards address organizational support for professional learning. The school leadership team supports professional learning that improves student learning by:

- Developing **learning communities** within the school that focus on continuous professional learning while providing structures and opportunities to support that learning;

- Building **leadership** capacity that distributes leadership responsibilities throughout the school focused on continuous improvement; and

- Using appropriate **resources**, such as time, to support different professional learning formats and activities embedded in the school day.

PROCESS STANDARDS

Process standards focus on how professional learning is identified, designed, and delivered. It is the *how* of professional learning. The school leadership team plans, implements, and evaluates professional learning that improves student learning by:

- Using disaggregated **data** to determine what educators need to learn, monitoring progress, and helping sustain continuous improvement;

- **Evaluating** the impact of professional learning on teacher effectiveness and student achievement for continuous improvement;

- Using **research** when deciding a content focus for professional learning;

- **Designing** professional learning using a variety of professional learning formats to accomplish the intended goals;

- Applying knowledge of adult **learning** and change processes when designing professional learning; and

- Developing **collaborative skills** so team members can effectively work together to improve teaching and learning.

CONTENT STANDARDS

Content standards identify the knowledge, skills, and attitudes teachers need in order for students to attain high levels of achievement. Content is the *what* of professional learning. The school leadership team determines content-focused professional learning that improves student learning by:

- Focusing on **equity** so that all students are understood and appreciated in a supportive learning environment with high expectations for everyone;

- Increasing **quality teaching** by having teachers deepen their content knowledge, learning, and application of research-based instructional strategies, and helping teachers learn to use a variety of classroom assessments; and

- Focusing on gaining knowledge and skills to **involve families** and other stakeholders appropriately.

*(**Tool 1.3** at the end of this chapter details each of the standards named in bold above.)*

The school leadership team's initial role is to plan and monitor implementation of school-based professional learning that is focused on improving instruction so student learning improves. The school leadership team builds school capacity by building teachers' capacity.

Focused, quality professional learning centered at the school and embedded into the daily activities of teaching contributes to changing instructional practices and impacts student performance. Providing ongoing professional learning at the school site means

> The fundamental purpose of the school leadership team is to determine the school's professional learning plan and identify the goals, priorities, and strategies to help implement that plan.

that teachers engage in learning during the workday. For such job-embedded learning to occur, the school leadership team creates and often facilitates learning teams or learning communities within the school. The school leadership team may recommend structures for learning teams and also helps hold teachers accountable for focusing on student performance.

To ensure that teachers engage in high-quality professional learning, school leadership team members attend to the context, process, and content standards for professional learning. The school leadership team's work, centered on professional learning, should align with standards for high-quality professional development.

The National Staff Development Council's Standards for Staff Development are divided among context, process, and content standards.

Context standards address organizational support for professional learning. The school leadership team supports professional learning that improves student learning by:

- Developing **learning communities** within the school that focus on continuous professional learning while providing structures and opportunities to support that learning;
- Building **leadership** capacity that distributes leadership responsibilities throughout the school focused on continuous improvement; and
- Using appropriate **resources,** such as time, to support different professional learning formats and activities embedded in the school day.

Process standards focus on how professional learning is identified, designed, and delivered. It is the "how" of professional learning. The school leadership team plans, implements, and evaluates professional learning that improves student learning by:

- Using disaggregated **data** to determine what educators need to learn, monitoring progress, and helping sustain continuous improvement;
- **Evaluating** the impact of professional learning on teacher effectiveness and student achievement for continuous improvement;
- Using **research** when deciding a content focus for professional learning;
- **Designing** professional learning using a variety of professional learning formats to accomplish the intended goals;
- Applying knowledge of adult **learning** and change processes when designing professional learning; and
- Developing **collaborative skills** so team members can effectively work together to

improve teaching and learning.

Content standards identify the knowledge, skills, and attitudes teachers need in order for students to attain high levels of achievement. Content is the "what" of professional learning. The school leadership team determines content-focused professional learning that improves student learning by:

- Focusing on **equity** so that all students are understood and appreciated in a supportive learning environment with high expectations for everyone;
- Increasing **quality teaching** by having teachers deepen their content knowledge, learning, and application of research-based instructional strategies, and helping teachers learn to use a variety of classroom assessments; and
- Focusing on gaining knowledge and skills to **involve families** and other stakeholders appropriately.

(**Tool 1.3** details each of the standards named in bold above.)

SELECTING TEAM MEMBERS

The school leader develops a school leadership team by carefully selecting and nurturing teacher leaders to ensure their collective focus on student achievement through planning, implementing, and evaluating high-quality professional learning aligned with district and school improvement goals.

McKeever and the California School Leadership Academy (2003, p. 52) identified criteria to use in selecting teachers to serve on the leadership team. Criteria include the teacher's:

- Respect for and influence among his or her colleagues;
- Knowledge and leadership capacity;
- Unique or specialized perspective that he or she would bring to the team;
- Grade-level or content-area expertise;
- Specialized training (e.g. special education, reading, English language development);
- Relationships with key members of the staff;
- Sense of the history, traditions, and context of the school;
- Aspiration to become an administrator; and
- Ability to lend balance to the makeup of the team.

Part of identifying effective members is defining the knowledge, attitudes, and skills members will need. The principal can use a description of desired knowledge, attitudes, and

Where to begin

▶ Develop a rationale to use with faculty and other stakeholders for why the school needs a leadership team and how the leadership team differs from other teams. Use this chapter and additional resources listed at the end of the chapter to help you.

▶ Help school staff clearly define what a school leadership team is and does, its role as a catalyst in school improvement and building capacity, and why someone would want or need to become a member of the leadership team. Use **Tool 1.1** to help potential members understand the breadth and depth of their role.

▶ Identify team members. Use **Tool 1.2** to help assess the qualities of different candidates.

skills, described in **Tool 1.1**, to assist in selecting members or to help determine what ongoing professional learning team members will need to continue their growth.

The personalities of those being considered may be another factor to consider. Michael Muir (2006) cites studies that indicate a group of diverse personalities is more effective and says some typical roles include the definer (creates the team's reality), analyst (explores and maps the team's reality), interpreter (predicts what others are likely to see), critic (redefines, reanalyzes, and reinterprets the team's reality),

synthesizer (orchestrates what the team knows), disparity monitor (gauges what outsiders think), task monitor (keeps the team on course), and emotional monitor (remembers emotions).

Although teachers sometimes are assigned to the leadership team, the school leader typically asks for volunteer teacher leaders willing to serve as members of the school leadership team and to recognize the new knowledge and skills they will need to perform such a role. Marzano et al. (2005) recommend that members of a school leadership team be volunteers. The rationale for working

Additional resources

Fullan, M. (2001). *Leading in a culture of change.* San Francisco: Jossey-Bass.

Fullan, M. (2001). *The new meaning of educational change* (3rd ed.). New York: Teachers College Press.

Garmston, R. & Wellman, B. (1999). *The adaptive school: A sourcebook for developing collaborative groups.* Norwood, MA: Christopher-Gordon.

Hall, G.E. & Hord, S.M. (1986). *Implementing change: Patterns, principles, and potholes.* Boston: Allyn & Bacon.

Hall, G.E. & Hord, S.M. *Configurations of school-based leadership teams.* Austin, TX: The University of Texas, Research and Development Center for Teacher Education. Available at www.eric.ed.gov/ERICWebPortal/recordDetail?accno=ED297415.

Hergert, L.F. (1997, Summer). Turning diversity into a strength for decision making. *Journal of Staff Development, 18*(3), 12-15.

Lambert, L. (2002, May). A framework for shared leadership. *Educational Leadership, 59*(8), 37-40.

Reeves, D. (2006). *The learning leader: How to focus school improvement for better results.* Alexandria, VA: ASCD.

with teachers who volunteer to be on the leadership team is that they probably have an "extraordinary commitment to the effective functioning of the school" (p. 104).

The size of the team varies between five and 12 members. The team should include representatives from each grade level or department. Equal representation from all grade-level or department learning teams allows communication to flow to and from the school leadership team to ensure the faculty's collective focus on professional learning embedded into teachers' daily work.

Participation on the leadership team often rotates, and members remain for a designated number of years. Three years on the team, for example, allows teachers to develop

relationships within the team and provides consistency in what members learn and transfer to grade-level teams or department learning teams. Understanding the leadership team's role and responsibilities will help in determining who should serve and for how long.

The work of leadership team members is ongoing and more comprehensive than that of other groups, such as the school improvement team. The leadership team will allow more individuals within the school to develop their talents. Recognizing the effect the team's work may have on adult learning and student achievement, teachers may be inspired to try on new roles and develop the skills to collaborate with and lead peers as they take on responsibility for school improvement.

Tools index

TOOL	TITLE	USE
1.1	Knowledge, attitudes, and skills needed as team members	**Tool 1.1** will help the principal and teacher leaders identify their strengths and focus areas for learning as the school's representatives.
1.2	Selecting team members	**Tool 1.2** will help the principal ensure the team has representatives from different learning teams in order to increase communication, facilitation, and monitoring of progress throughout the school.
1.3	NSDC's Standards for Staff Development	**Tool 1.3** defines each of NSDC's 12 standards for high-quality professional development that improves teaching and student learning.
1.4	NSDC Tool: Assessing your role as instructional leader	**Tool 1.4** will help the principal determine how his or her behavior aligns with the behavior of a strong instructional leader.

"The most important feature of an educator is to
provide the conditions under which people's learning
curves go off the chart. Sometimes it is the other
people's learning curves: those of students, teachers,
parents, administrators. But at all times, it is our own
learning curve."

— Roland Barth, "The leader as learner,"
Education Week, March 5, 1997

Chapter 2

LEARNING
to lead

Becoming an effective member of a school leadership team takes specific knowledge and skills. Members first need to understand their roles and responsibilities as part of the leadership team. Team members need also to develop a more system-level perspective. To broaden their understanding, team members should study the definition of high-quality professional development to clarify their purpose and should learn more about change as a process, for themselves and for colleagues with whom they will be working. Another aspect of teaming is learning to use joint time efficiently and effectively. The essentials of effective meetings also are core understandings for members of any effective team.

UNDERSTANDING LEADERSHIP TEAM MEMBERS' ROLES AND RESPONSIBILITIES

The crucial role of a member on the school leadership team is to be an effective teacher leader. As Stephen Covey (2010) notes, "Leadership is the highest of all the arts, for it is the enabling art of unlocking human potential. It is communicating to people their worth and potential so clearly that they come to see it in themselves."

The leadership team's ultimate responsibility is to develop others' potential. To unlock the potential in others, team members begin with themselves, developing an understanding of how they will go about their work.

Members of a school leadership team can define their responsibilities by aligning their roles with NSDC's Standards for Staff Development. By beginning to define their roles

DESIRED OUTCOMES

The leadership team should align the school-based professional learning with NSDC's Standards for Staff Development. The following desired outcomes for the leadership team are identified on the Innovation Configuration map for NSDC's Quality Teaching standard, which should help leadership team members align their work with teachers with the standard (Roy & Hord, 2003, p. 20).

These outcomes describe the highest level on the IC map for leadership teams. The leadership team:	▶ **Contributes to planning school-based professional learning.** ▶ **Articulates the intended results of staff development programs on teacher practice.** ▶ **Articulates the benefits of professional learning.** ▶ **Engages in professional development that considers participant concerns about new practices.**

in this way, they also will ensure that plans for professional learning align with the standards.

These essential skills and practices for leading school improvement efforts align with NSDC's Standards for Staff Development.

- **Learning Communities:** Create and maintain a collaborative school culture through learning communities to monitor continuous progress.
- **Leadership:** Involve the faculty in planning and implementing high-quality professional learning at the school level.
- **Resources:** Align time, structures, personnel, and materials to support professional growth.
- **Data-Driven:** Use disaggregated student data to identify adult learning priorities for professional learning included in the school improvement plan.
- **Evaluation:** Use formative and summative evaluation to measure the impact of school-based professional learning.

- **Research-Based:** Develop capacity to use research to support schoolwide instructional decisions.
- **Design:** Facilitate and support ongoing, in-depth, and sustained professional learning opportunities embedded in the school day.
- **Learning:** Understand and apply knowledge about the change process when planning and implementing professional learning.
- **Collaboration:** Facilitate learning experiences where staff learn how to work collaboratively with colleagues and collectively are responsible for student learning.
- **Equity:** Establish a safe school environment with high expectations for all students and adults.
- **Quality Teaching:** Focus content of professional learning on curriculum, instruction, and assessment.
- **Family Involvement:** Involve parents and community in discussions and activities

related to school improvement.

Leadership team members review these skills and identify areas where they may need to develop their abilities as they prepare to work with colleagues. These teacher leaders also need a clear understanding of how their work will be accomplished through organizing professional learning, beginning with developing their understanding of what constitutes effective professional learning.

UNDERSTANDING HIGH-QUALITY PROFESSIONAL LEARNING

To lead colleagues in a collective focus on improving student learning, the school leadership team needs a clear understanding

---

These essential skills and practices for leading school improvement efforts align with NSDC's Standards for Staff Development.

- **Learning Communities:** Create and maintain a collaborative school culture through learning communities to monitor continuous progress.

- **Leadership:** Involve the faculty in planning and implementing high-quality professional learning at the school level.

- **Resources:** Align time, structures, personnel, and materials to support professional growth.

- **Data-Driven:** Use disaggregated student data to identify adult learning priorities for professional learning included in the school improvement plan.

- **Evaluation:** Use formative and summative evaluation to measure the impact of school-based professional learning.

- **Research-Based:** Develop capacity to use research to support schoolwide instructional decisions.

- **Design:** Facilitate and support ongoing, in-depth, and sustained professional learning opportunities embedded in the school day.

- **Learning:** Understand and apply knowledge about the change process when planning and implementing professional learning.

- **Collaboration:** Facilitate learning experiences where staff learn how to work collaboratively with colleagues and collectively are responsible for student learning.

- **Equity:** Establish a safe school environment with high expectations for all students and adults.

- **Quality Teaching:** Focus content of professional learning on curriculum, instruction, and assessment.

- **Family Involvement:** Involve parents and community in discussions and activities related to school improvement.

"that high-quality professional development improves the learning of all students by continuously improving the day-to-day practices of teachers and educational leaders. It does so by promoting deep understanding of subject matter content, expanding teachers' repertoires of research-based strategies, affecting educators' beliefs about teaching and learning through dialogue and other methods, and stimulating a steady stream of goal-focused actions" (Sparks, 2004, p. 2).

Team members' knowledge of high-quality professional learning will affect their ability to plan, implement, and evaluate professional learning at the school. To begin, members need to understand and be able to apply a definition of high-quality professional learning.

NSDC advocates for a new definition of professional development based on the need for high-quality professional development for every educator. NSDC's Standards for Staff Development (NSDC, 2001) were built on three underlying principles — that professional learning should be results-driven, standards-based, and job-embedded.

- **Results-driven** means beginning with a clear and specific goal that describes teacher and student learning and then planning backward to accomplish that goal.
- **Standards-based** refers to four sets of standards that fuel effective staff development: student content standards, teaching standards, leadership standards, and staff development standards. These standards inform staff development content so student learning improves.
- **Job-embedded** means that teachers engage in ongoing learning during the school day within their work setting and suggests that professional learning becomes a routine component of every teacher's workday. Job-embedded professional development revolves around conversing with colleagues, examining student work, jointly planning

lessons, observing classrooms, and solving problems with colleagues. All these activities not only improve educators' professional knowledge and skill but also affect student learning. (Roy & Hord, 2004, p. 57). Job-embedded learning requires different planning and facilitating.

Leadership team members must clearly understand the link between professional learning and school goals, and what constitutes quality professional learning. **Tool 2.1** is a report by Darling-Hammond, Wei, Andree, Richardson, and Orphanos (2009) about effective teacher development and trends and strategies abroad. The authors state (p. 7), "Professional learning can have a powerful effect on teacher skills and knowledge and on student learning if it is sustained over time, focused on important content, and embedded in the work of professional learning communities that support ongoing improvements in teachers' practice."

Once members have studied tools and resources about quality professional learning and its effects, they will be ready to explain its importance to colleagues. As team members lead colleagues in professional learning, they also must understand that change can be exciting for some, challenging for most, and threatening for a few people.

UNDERSTANDING CHANGE

To lead change that uses high-quality professional learning to build a school faculty's capacity to improve student achievement, team members develop their understanding of the characteristics of first- and second-order change, which "distinguish between changes that are: 1) an extension of past practice versus a break with past practice; 2) consistent versus inconsistent with prevailing organizational norms; 3) congruent versus incongruent with personal values; and 4) implemented with existing knowledge and skills versus requiring new knowledge and skills" (Dean, Galvin, & Parsley, 2005, p. 3).

Key points in professional development

High-quality professional learning:

- Fosters collective responsibility.

- Is conducted among educators at the school.

- Is facilitated by well-prepared school principals and/or school-based teacher leaders.

- Occurs several times per week.

- Engages educators in a continuous cycle of school improvement.

- Identifies student, teacher, and school learning needs.

- Defines educator learning goals based on needs.

- Provides job-embedded coaching or assistance to support transfer of learning to the classroom.

- Regularly assesses effectiveness of professional development in achieving identified learning goals, improving teaching, and assisting all students in achieving standards.

Source: Hirsh, 2009.

Order refers to the degree of change. (Marzano, Waters, & McNulty, 2005). First-order change means maintaining status quo. Teachers continue to rely on their existing knowledge and skills. Second-order change requires teachers to gain new knowledge and skills and try new approaches in their classrooms. Second-order change may cause conflict, challenges, and discomfort.

At this stage, leadership team members become more educated about how adults react to the possibilities of change and how perceptions of change vary. The resources provided with this chapter help to begin conversations about objections facing leadership teams, feelings team members might experience, and an overview of the process of change. As the team begins to develop specific plans for school-based professional learning, members will create a theory of change that is more specific about

their understanding. Reading and learning about how people experience change is the first, early stage of beginning to think about human needs in processing new learning.

Tools 2.10 and **2.11** will help leadership team members understand more about the Concerns-Based Adoption Model (CBAM) and be able to measure teachers' concern to use in planning professional development.

UNDERSTANDING THE BASICS OF TEAMWORK

When team members understand their roles and responsibilities as teacher leaders, as well as how change occurs and the role of high-quality professional learning, they are ready to begin their work. Working in a team, however, requires having clear outcomes in mind in order to achieve the team's goals. A few early essentials for working effectively in a group include the ability to focus clearly on the work at hand, to fill key functions on the team, to develop efficient working norms for the group, and to make decisions as a group.

Setting agendas.

As the team meets, one litmus test that will help ascertain progress is the team's meeting agenda. Setting an agenda is more than making a list. A good agenda requires thoughtful planning. Planning is an essential component to organizing and running a successful meeting. Preparation, reflected first in the agenda, is a key to productivity.

Who will set the agenda? For a school leadership team, the principal may initiate the first agenda, and the role then may rotate to allow multiple members to share responsibility and grow in their own knowledge. The same person may take on the task for several meetings in a row before the role rotates to another. The group as a whole may decide at the end of each meeting what to cover in the next meeting. In some teams, one person may

be designated to set the agenda.

Ann Delehant (2007) states that the meeting content can be decided:

- Based on the group's stated purpose and identified needs;
- Based on participants' input before the meeting;
- By group members at the beginning of a meeting or the end of the prior meeting;
- Based on prior meeting minutes; or
- A combination of the above.

Each meeting should have clearly stated objectives. After the meeting content is determined, members can decide how long to meet, where to meet, and when. All of the logistical information may be included on the agenda to allow members to refer to it easily.

Delehant (2007, p. 17) says an agenda should include:

- **Topic.** A brief description of the issue or item to be discussed.
- **Responsible person.** The person who will lead the discussion of the topic. This does not imply the person who will manage the

---

Basics of understanding change

Joellen Killion and Pat Roy, in *Becoming a Learning School* (NSDC, 2009, pp. 46-48), say understanding change requires understanding these basics:

- People respond differently to change.

- Change can cause divisiveness.

- Conflict is a natural part of change.

- Change is a process.

- Too many changes can derail all improvement efforts.

- Organizations change only if the people in them change.

initiative; it does acknowledge the person who will facilitate the process during the meeting.

- **Desired outcome.** The goal or purpose so that the facilitator and team members clearly understand what must be accomplished. This is the most important element of the agenda. The desired outcome is written as a neutral statement, not one to predict or predetermine the outcome of the discussion. For example, the desired outcome statement would not be "Approve offering university credit for conference attendance." Instead, it would be phrased, "Determine whether to offer university credit for conference attendance."

- **Timeline.** The amount of time allotted to the issue. To keep the group on task, reference the actual hour and minutes rather than a generic number of minutes. For example, write "9:45 a.m. to 10 a.m." rather than "15 minutes." The clock will keep the group on target, whereas the number of minutes can lead to sloppy timekeeping. Using hours will also help the team determine the meeting's length and decide whether to break up the work over more than one session.

- **Member involvement.** Notations identifying the expected involvement from group members. For example, (I) might indicate an information item, (D) discussion/dialogue items, (A) action item, or (DP) decision point. Items might be grouped together under a heading on the agenda.

Delehant recommends carefully considering the sequence of items to pace the meeting, and that the person responsible for the agenda send it to each group member 24 hours to 48 hours ahead of the meeting, depending on members' preference.

Members also may find it helpful to have a draft to review before the final agenda is sent so that they can offer feedback to clarify, focus, or add to the agenda items. Without this input, the agenda may have to include some flexible time for attendees to raise other issues. Have a deadline for input to ensure that the final agenda goes out in time before the meeting.

The primary issue is to be sure the focus of the work is clear, and creating the agenda will help to determine whether that is the case.

Determining members' roles within the team.

"Team members need a sense of where they fit into traditional team responsibilities," according to Anne Jolly (2008, p. 68). Jolly notes that individuals should take time to reflect on their roles and how they work collectively. She recommends that the team spend a brief time answering:

- Who are we as a team?
- What is our purpose?
- Who do we need to be to accomplish that purpose?

Answering these questions, she says, keeps energy and productivity high when they may flag.

Most teams will have members serving a variety of roles over the course of the group's work. Some teams rotate the roles, while others may have some members remain in a few key roles for longer periods to provide stability. Rotating roles allows all members to develop their skills in different areas. However, consider carefully how frequently roles are rotated to provide the group with the benefit of more individuals with developed knowledge and skill.

Delehant (2007) recommends that after the group reviews possible roles and decides which are needed, the group should at the outset specify the length of time that each member will fill a role and determine if any mentoring might be of value. The group chair or facilitator may simply assign roles for the first round at the group's initial meeting, Delehant says (2007).

Groups working together typically have several common roles within the team:

Agenda builder. This person is responsible for gathering input and putting together the group's wishes for the agenda. The agenda builder does not unilaterally create the agenda. He or she makes sure that all members have been heard and that all receive the agenda ahead of the meeting. The skill in creating the agenda involves placing items in an appropriate order that maximizes efficiency, i.e. pacing the agenda.

Facilitator. A good facilitator helps members determine their goals and how to get there, then makes sure the work is accomplished. The facilitator may paraphrase, summarize, probe, push, redirect, test the group's understanding, coach, build consensus, and otherwise assist the group in its work, but usually is not directly involved in offering advice or opinions as an active group member would. This position is that of a guide rather than contributor.

In the absence of a team leader, the facilitator often also functions as the person responsible for arranging a meeting place and assisting with other necessary meeting details.

This is an essential role on a working leadership team and may be filled by a team member or an external expert with the requisite skill.

Recorder. This person keeps the minutes of the meetings, recording the group's efforts and results. The team may use a log to help the group communicate its learning to other key stakeholders within the school, whether the principal, other teacher groups, or the faculty as a whole. The recorder should be able to detail the group's work accurately, clearly, and concisely, including key decisions. This is an essential role that should be filled.

Scribe. In some meetings, the group may want to chart a running record of the conversation in order to work from those notes during the meeting. The scribe is usually a volunteer who fulfills this function on an as-needed basis. Clear handwriting, an ability to synthesize the conversation and distill ideas, and a willingness to clarify points are essential skills.

Timekeeper. The timekeeper reminds the group of how much meeting time remains and where the group is on the agenda, as needed. The timekeeper should intervene only when necessary to ask the team how members may want to proceed if time is getting short. The timekeeper's observations may also be useful in setting future agendas as the team gets a sense of how long it spends on certain actions or activities.

Observer. The team may occasionally want feedback on how it is functioning in order to facilitate the work. An observer who sits outside the group to see how members interact and how work is accomplished can produce useful insights. Delehant (2007, p. 70) notes that the observer might look for members' preparation, participation, leadership, roles, ability to make decisions, communication, sensitivity, and any other noticeable group attributes. The observer provides feedback on how well group members work together and may make recommendations for improvement.

Group member. Every member of the team is an essential part of the team. The function of the group member is to actively contribute to the group, participate in discussion, offer thoughtful opinions, and provide the group with the benefit of his or her knowledge and skill as an active contributor.

Developing norms.

Groups work better together when all members understand the expectations of the group. If, for example, the group does not begin meetings on time and one member consistently arrives later than others, others may be irritated with the latecomer but not see how a clear-cut norm — meetings will begin and end on time — would remedy the situation. With generational and cultural differences in faculties, norms help bridge gaps in experiences, expectations, and what "feels right" to different people. Discussing expectations and coming to agreement on common criteria help build a sense of one another from the beginning of the team's existence, so creating norms is a valuable exercise in and of itself in addition to setting a tone for subsequent meetings.

Norms should be clearly posted during meetings and members reminded to refer to the list as one of their responsibilities on the team to keep the work on track. Rather than calling attention to an individual, for example, a group member may refer to the norm and remind the group of members' agreements to follow these expectations.

Reaching decisions.

Teacher leaders also will need to know how to reach decisions as a group. The best way to reach group decisions is through consensus, working through discussions that reveal all members' issues, developing a common view on problems or obstacles, and deciding on the best possible course of action as the group as a whole sees it. **Tools 2.7** to **2.9** can help with understanding consensus.

Team member responsibilities

- Come prepared to meetings.
- Complete assignments in a timely manner.
- Develop the agenda in an open and systematic manner.
- Initiate an agenda item in a way that opens discussion.
- Seek information in an open and nonthreatening manner.
- Give information that contributes to the knowledge and decision-making process.
- Offer opinions as opinions, not as facts.
- Elaborate on another's contribution.
- Combine ideas from two or more participants into one stronger idea.
- Energize the group when necessary.
- Use different decision-making and problem-solving strategies as appropriate.
- Encourage participation from all members.
- Find common ground between contrary opinions.
- Give and be open to feedback on the impact of various types of behavior and the impact on the group.
- Remind the group of its commitments to fairness, openness, and respect.
- Ask to examine group effectiveness at key intervals.
- Acknowledge individuals' contributions to the group.

Source: Delehant, 2007, p. 50.

Sample norms

- Begin and end meetings on time.
- Come prepared to the meeting.
- Be quiet when another person is speaking.
- Listen carefully to one another.
- Keep confidential issues in confidence.
- Treat one another with respect.
- Keep discussions impersonal.
- State assumptions.
- Be open to all points of view and examine others' opinions.
- Own the group's decision.
- Be accountable for your commitments.
- Strive to continuously improve.
- Reach for agreement on what is best for the whole (team/school), rather than an individual.
- Practice active listening.

Where to begin

▶ Develop a clear understanding of members' roles and responsibilities as part of the leadership team. **Tool 2.2** will help in this work.

▶ Learn the key points of high-quality professional development. Use **Tool 2.3** to understand NSDC's definition.

▶ Spend time studying the change process, both for team members' clarity and to prepare to work with colleagues. Use **Tools 2.10** and **2.11**.

▶ Review some of the basics of group work. Use additional resources to learn about efficient meetings, collaboration and consensus, stages of teamwork, and other aspects of teaming.

Additional resources

Conzemius, A. & O'Neill, J. (2002). *The handbook for SMART school teams.* Bloomington, IN: Solution Tree.

Darling-Hammond, L. & Richardson, N. (2009, February). Teacher learning: What matters? *Educational Leadership, 66*(5), 46-53.

Delehant, A. (with von Frank, V.). (2007). *Making meetings work: How to get started, get going, and get it done.* Thousand Oaks, CA: Corwin Press with NSDC.

Gallimore, R., Ermeling, B., Saunders, W., & Goldenberg, C. (2009, May). Moving the learning of teaching closer to practice: Teacher education implications of school-based inquiry teams. *The Elementary School Journal, 109*(5), 537-553.

Hall, G.E. & Hord, S.M. (1986). *Implementing change: Patterns, principles, and potholes.* Boston: Allyn & Bacon.

Jolly, A. (2008). *Team to teach: A facilitator's guide to professional learning teams.* Oxford, OH: NSDC.

National Staff Development Council. (2001). *NSDC's standards for staff development.* Oxford, OH: Author.

Reeves, D. (2010). *Transforming professional development into student results.* Alexandria, VA: ASCD.

Roy, P. & Hord, S. (2003). *Moving NSDC's staff development standards into practice: Innovation Configurations.* Oxford, OH: NSDC & SEDL.

Roy, P. & Hord, S. (2004, Spring). Innovation Configurations chart a measured course toward change. *JSD, 25*(2), 54-58.

Tools index

TOOL	TITLE	USE
2.1	Professional learning study and Save the Last Word for Me protocol	**Tool 2.1** is a report summarizing key findings about professional development in the United States and other countries and can be used in discussions of how the school's current practices compare with what research shows is effective in strengthening teacher quality and student achievement. A protocol helps engage faculty in identifying strengths and areas for improving professional learning. This tool includes the Save the Last Word for Me protocol to use in reading the report.
2.2	Roles and responsibilities of school leadership team members	**Tool 2.2** will help team members identify their level of understanding of their role, their need for professional development, and the support they need to meet their responsibilities.
2.3	A definition of high-quality professional development	**Tool 2.3** outlines a proposed amendment to [Section 9101 (34)] of the Elementary and Secondary Education Act. Use this definition to develop district policy and align the school's professional learning. An accompanying video clip showing the definition in practice is also available.
2.4	Leadership self-assessment questionnaire	**Tool 2.4** helps team members assess their perceptions of the leadership team's effectiveness. Compile individual results to identify similarities and differences in perceptions, and use the results to guide continuous improvement.
2.5	Assessment of leadership team indicators	**Tool 2.5** can be used to assess members' perceptions of how the team is functioning compared with specific leadership indicators. Compile individual results and look for trends to guide continuous improvement.

Tools index

TOOL	TITLE	USE
2.6	Characteristics of high-performing schools	**Tool 2.6** defines characteristics of high-performing schools and helps deepen leadership team members' understanding of attributes that are school goals.
2.7	General directions for reaching consensus	**Tool 2.7** will help the group reach an understanding of what should be done and how, with all agreeing to support the group's decision.
2.8	Consensus: Tap into a powerful decision-making tool	**Tool 2.8** provides the leadership team with steps to reach consensus and describes what happens when consensus can't be reached. Use the information when working within the leadership team, with faculty, and with collaborative teams.
2.9	Consensus: Arrive at agreement — agreeably	**Tool 2.9** provides the leadership team with information about a process for working together which includes three phases (preparation, possibilities, probing). All groups at the school (leadership team, faculty, collaborative teams) should set expectations for how members will work together to reach consensus.
2.10	Concerns-Based Adoption Model	**Tool 2.10** explains this conceptual framework that predicts teacher behaviors throughout the school change process. Includes tools 7 Stages of Concern and Levels of Use.
2.11	Research-based tool gauges actual use of a new approach	**Tool 2.11** describes typical Levels of Use of new initiatives to help leadership team members deepen their understanding of putting learning into practice.

"Job-embedded professional development refers
to teacher learning that is grounded in day-to-day
teaching practice and is designed to enhance teachers'
content-specific instructional practices with the intent
of improving student learning."

— Andrew Croft, Jane Coggshall, Megan Dolan, and
Elizabeth Powers, *Job-Embedded Professional
Development: What It Is, Who Is Responsible, and How
to Get It Done Well*, 2010

Chapter 3

PLANNING
school-based professional learning

The school leadership team's purpose is to develop colleagues' abilities to raise student achievement. Developing teachers' instructional capacity requires quality professional learning. Therefore, school leadership teams are responsible for designing what teacher learning will look like and how best to implement the learning plan. Leadership team members examine the school's context to decide how best to support teacher learning and then help facilitate a professional learning plan.

As Pat Roy and Shirley Hord state (2004, p. 56):

- The goal of professional development is increased student learning.
- To achieve high levels of student learning,

teachers must develop new knowledge, skills, attitudes, and behaviors.
- Professional development must be planned, designed, and implemented in ways that increase educators' capacity to impact student learning.
- The organizational structures, policies, and practices must be aligned to support the professional development program and goals.

The school leadership team's role is to use a backmapping model that begins with engaging staff in identifying what students need to know and be able to do. With that information, the leadership team can determine what teachers need to know and then can design results-driven, standards-based, job-embedded professional learning that will focus on improving student achievement.

CHANGE, LEAD, SUCCEED

Figure 3.1: Backmapping model for planning results-based professional development

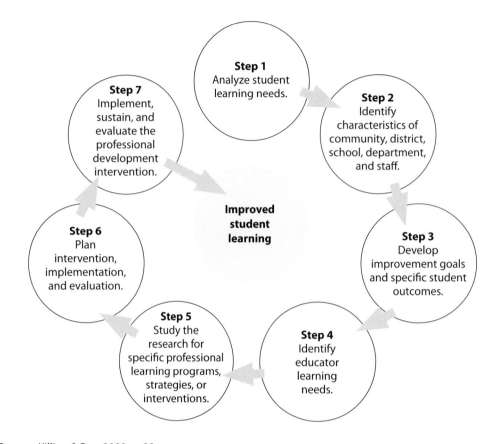

Source: Killion & Roy, 2009, p. 99.

The leadership team bases its work on three key questions:
- What do students need to know and be able to do?
- What do educators need to know and be able to do to ensure student success?
- What professional development will ensure educators acquire the necessary knowledge and skills?

Backmapping is essential to professional planning. According to Killion (2008, p. 212), backmapping "is a process for planning. This planning model is based on results and begins with the end in mind."

Figure 3.1 shows a backmapping model for planning results-based staff development (Killion & Roy, 2009). The steps for this model are explained in more detail in this chapter. Alternatives are available in **Tool 3.2**.

Killion notes that some steps may be similar to those in school improvement planning, in which the school improvement team identifies student needs, student learning goals, and the means to achieve them. "School improvement plans and professional learning should complement and be aligned with each other," she states (2008, p. 99). The leadership team uses the school improvement plan as a complementary resource for data analysis and to help structure its plans for professional learning.

STEP 1: ANALYZE STUDENT LEARNING NEEDS.

Teachers in many schools, especially teachers serving on school leadership teams, are relatively skilled at analyzing and interpreting student achievement data. The leadership team analyzes student achievement data from multiple sources of data (standardized test scores, grades, teacher observations, formative assessments, other student data) to identify strengths and areas of need, cross-referencing among the data to get a sense of the most urgent areas to target.

Leadership team members should gather and analyze data to be able to point to specific areas of student achievement and areas of student need. Areas of achievement are helpful to use to point out to faculty what teachers are doing well and to celebrate the positive. Close inspection of strengths also can possibly yield some ideas of teacher skills that could transfer to other areas. For example, if an analysis of data reveals that 1st-grade teachers are particularly strong in teaching students to decode words in language arts, but 3rd-grade reading scores are not exceptional, the 1st-grade teachers may have some skills and knowledge that would help their colleagues in 2nd and 3rd grades continue to build on students' strengths in decoding.

Data analysis results in knowing or identifying:
- Specific areas of student need;
- Specific knowledge and skills that students need in order to improve achievement; and
- Specific students or groups of students

Key questions to answer during this step include:

- What assessment data are available?
- What is being measured in each assessment?
- What areas of student performance are meeting or exceeding expectations?
- What areas of student performance are below expectations?
- What patterns exist within the data? How are the data similar or different in various grade levels, content areas, and individual classes?
- How did various groups of students perform? (Consider gender, race, special needs, English language learners, and socioeconomic status.)
- What do other data reveal about student performance?
- How are the data similar or different in various grade levels, content areas, and individual classes?
- What surprises us?
- What confirms what we already know?

Source: Killion & Roy, 2009.

for whom the need is most prevalent or pronounced (Killion & Roy, 2009, p. 100).

Once the team identifies specific areas of need and has prioritized needs, leadership team members may focus on determining what skills teachers need to have to be able to target the identified student needs.

To be able to focus on teacher skills, the identified need must be specific. Identifying a weakness in science, for example, is not helpful. On the other hand, stating that 5th-grade students are not showing evidence of understanding friction and gravity can lead the team to being able to investigate specifically the skills needed to improve teaching those topics and design focused, ongoing professional learning at the school site.

The school leadership team initially is responsible for analyzing data. After team members have outlined student and teacher needs based on data, the team next facilitates the process with the whole faculty during faculty meetings or with grade-level or department teams in learning team meetings so that teachers have a deeper understanding and knowledge of the basis for the identified needs and targeted skills.

STEP 2: IDENTIFY CHARACTERISTICS OF COMMUNITY, DISTRICT, SCHOOL, DEPARTMENT, AND STAFF.

To design appropriate professional learning and follow-up support, the school leadership team should know not only the characteristics of the students in the school, but also the characteristics of the adult learners. Professional learning design should consider adult characteristics, such as the number of new versus experienced teachers, years in the school, and years at a grade level. Resources, such as time, people, and funding, will impact professional learning as well.

The leadership team gathers data to develop a school profile (Killion & Roy, 2009, p. 101). Key questions to ask in this area are:

- What are the characteristics of our students?
- What are the characteristics of the staff?
- What are some characteristics of our formal and informal leadership for both teachers and administrators?
- What are some characteristics of our community?
- What resources are available to support professional development?

Some staff characteristics to consider include: experience level, years at grade level, years in the school, performance, attitude, education level, gender, age/generation, educational background, sense of efficacy, understanding of professional learning.

Some leadership characteristics to consider include: leadership style, roles of formal and informal leaders, participation in leadership activities, trust in leadership, opportunities to lead, support by leadership, support for leadership, level of communication.

Characteristics of the community might include: level of support for education and for the school, parental and community member involvement in school activities, support for professional learning.

An analysis of these data will help determine the most appropriate interventions for the school context.

STEP 3: DEVELOP IMPROVEMENT GOALS AND SPECIFIC STUDENT OUTCOMES.

The leadership team sets clear, measurable outcomes for school-based professional learning. The leadership team is careful to ensure that the intended results of the professional learning are stated and the outcome is an effect on student achievement.

Key questions to ask about the outcome are:

- What results do we seek for students? What do they need to know and be able to do?

- What results do we expect for staff? What do educators need to know and be able to do to ensure student success?
- What practices, procedures, and policies will affect our ability to achieve these goals? What professional development will ensure educators acquire the necessary knowledge and skills (Killion, 2002, p. 151)?

According to Conzemius and O'Neill (2002, p. 244), most educators state goals in terms of process rather than results. Process goals tend to "focus on the activities, programs, strategies, and methods that educators want to engage in. … Results goals answer the 'so what' question: So what if we did all these things? What actual improvement would we expect or want to see?"

For example, a professional learning goal is not: "Every staff person will be a member of a professional learning community." A professional learning goal will identify the specific actions, learning, and student achievement outcomes intended. Professional learning for teachers and principals is the means to achieve the goal of increased student achievement, so extend the traditional student achievement goal to include the end result of professional learning.

The goals the school leadership team sets go beyond those in the school improvement plan. For example, the school improvement goal might be to improve student reading scores by a certain percentage over a specific number of years. As the leadership team analyzes data, members dig deeper and find that most students are scoring lower in reading comprehension. Analyzing data further and considering multiple sources, team members home in on inference as the skill with which most students struggle. A professional development target, then, would be to increase reading comprehension by improving students' skills in making inferences.

The leadership team in this example might answer the guiding questions as follows:

1. What do students need to know and be able to do? Students need to improve their skills in making inferences.
2. What do educators need to know and

Using SMART goals to guide learning

According to Anne Conzemius and Jan O'Neill (2002, pp. 246-247), teachers who use SMART goals to guide their learning will:

- **Set** specific, measurable, learner-focused goals together.
- **Plan** how to help learners accomplish those goals.
- **Gather** evidence of individual and class progress toward the goal, analyze the trends over time, and compare results to exemplar schools as examples of best practices.
- **Share** their results.
- **Adjust** teaching strategies based on what they're learning together.
- **Develop** new plans for meeting their goals.

Examples of SMART goals

The purpose of professional development is to increase student achievement. Designing quality school-based professional learning starts with a SMART goal that identifies the desired result. SMART stands for specific, measurable, attainable, results-based, and time-bound (Killion, 2008, p. 36).

Examples of SMART goals:

- In three years, 90% of 3rd-grade students will read on grade level as a result of teachers learning and implementing new instructional strategies for word decoding.

- Within three years, 5% of all 5th through 8th graders will improve their mathematical problem solving as measured on the state assessment test and on school-based performance tasks as teachers learn and use strategies for integrating word problems into instruction.

be able to do to ensure student success? Teachers need to know and be able to teach students how to make inferences.

3. What professional development will ensure educators acquire the necessary knowledge and skills? The collective focus will be on learning how to teach students to make inferences, with the expectation that teachers will transfer their learning to the classrooms. Job-embedded team learning will involve theory, demonstration, practice, and coaching. The evaluation of the professional learning will include monitoring changes in teaching practices and student results in making inferences.

An improved learning goal might be, "Teachers use research-based instructional strategies to improve students' ability to make inferences from a text, resulting in an increase in student achievement in reading comprehension by 10% within two years."

As in the above example, learning goals should be stated as SMART goals (specific, measurable, attainable, results-based, and time-bound). McKeever (2003, p. 15) states:

"The goal is specific and therefore written in clear, simple language. The goal is measurable because it targets student achievement that can be quantified and, when necessary, uses multiple measures. The goal is realistic and therefore attainable. The goal is relevant because it is supported by a clear rationale and has been approved by the superintendent or his or her designee. A time frame for the achievement of the goal is clearly stated, making the goal time-bound."

It is important to dig deep enough into student achievement data to identify specific student needs. The leadership team will identify professional learning goals that are narrower than the goals outlined in a school improvement plan. The school improvement plan includes the staff's broad annual improvement goal or annual measurable objective and usually does not include a clear link between professional learning and the student achievement goal.

STEP 4: IDENTIFY EDUCATOR LEARNING NEEDS.

The next step is to identify what teachers need to know and be able to do to ensure student success in the area(s) of need. Identifying educator learning needs requires a shift in thinking, however. Identifying educators' needs is not the same as identifying what teachers think they need or what they would choose to learn about, which is the basis for much professional development. Effective professional learning for a school does not mean that teachers select individual courses from a catalogue of workshops or take part in site-based programs focused on the latest trend in educational strategies or on school procedures.

Providing quality professional learning requires a shift in thinking from conducting a needs assessment to determine what educators want to learn to identifying the skills they need to learn to meet identified areas of student need.

Continuing the example from Step 3, the leadership team will begin to determine how teachers instruct students in reading comprehension, specifically in how to make inferences from a text. By comparing teacher practices with identified best practices, team members can determine what skills staff lack. The next step will be to plan how best to help colleagues develop those skills. The school leadership team's role is to identify specific professional learning that will meet teachers' learning needs and help ensure that identified student needs are met and to work with teachers in planning which strategies to adopt. Once the team has identified the professional learning content, members will plan how learning will occur on site for teachers throughout the school year.

Questions that the leadership team needs to consider during this planning phase are:

- How will professional learning occur at the school site throughout the school year?
- What length and frequency will collective, ongoing learning opportunities have?
- How will the team ensure that trainers and facilitators use theory, demonstrations, and practice opportunities during school-based professional development?
- How will the leadership team ensure that

DESIRED OUTCOMES

The leadership team should align the school-based professional learning with NSDC's Standards for Staff Development. The following desired outcomes for the leadership team are identified on the Innovation Configuration map for NSDC's Data-Driven standard, which should help leadership team members in their work with teachers using data to design school-based professional learning.

These outcomes describe the highest level on the IC map for leadership teams. The leadership team:	▶ **Engages teachers in data analysis and interpretation to determine student and teacher needs.** ▶ **Designs professional learning that improves student achievement based on disaggregated data.**

learning teams (i.e. grade-level/department teams) meet regularly to share teacher practices and student results?

STEP 5: STUDY THE RESEARCH FOR SPECIFIC PROFESSIONAL LEARNING PROGRAMS, STRATEGIES, OR INTERVENTIONS.

Leadership team members need to become critical consumers of research to identify evidence-based instructional strategies that help improve student learning in the area of the identified need.

The leadership team reads studies related to the identified learning need, such as making inferences. The team selects studies that support practices addressing identified areas of need and leads the faculty in reading and discussing the strongest articles.

In evaluating a program described in an article, team members might ask:

- What was the research question? Were the authors trying to solve the same problem that we are?
- What were the study's results? Were they reported in effect sizes? Was the size of

the effect statistically significant and positive? In your opinion, were the benefits substantial?

- Compare the students in the study sample with our own. Has this strategy benefited other students in previous studies?
- Is this treatment practical for our faculty? Do we need or have access to trainers or external experts? Do we have time in our professional development schedule to learn these skills?
- Does the study describe teachers' actions? If yes, what are the actions (Iowa Department of Education, 2009)?

In examining programs, key questions to consider are:

- Which professional learning addresses the skills and knowledge we have identified as educator learning needs?
- What professional development are schools with similar demographics using?
- If our school's characteristics do not match the schools in which the professional learning was successful, what are the key differences? How likely is it that those differences will interfere with the program's

---

DESIRED OUTCOMES

The leadership team should align the school-based professional learning with NSDC's Standards for Staff Development. The following desired outcomes for the leadership team are identified on the Innovation Configuration map for NSDC's Data-Driven standard, which should help leadership team members in their work with teachers using data to design school-based professional learning.

These outcomes describe the highest level on the IC map for leadership teams. The leadership team:	▶ **Reads, critiques, and interprets educational research.** ▶ **Increases staff's capacity to analyze research to make instructional decisions.** ▶ **Engages the staff in using research to make informed instructional decisions.**

success? What changes might increase the likelihood of success?

- What are the strengths and weaknesses of the professional learning?
- What school, district, and community support was required to make the professional learning successful (Killion & Roy, 2009, p. 103)?

Two sources for critical evaluations are the Institute of Education Sciences (http://ies.ed.gov/) and NSDC's series of *What Works* books that reviewed professional development programs in various content areas for elementary, middle, and high school levels. The books provide each program's evidence of impact on student learning.

In examining the school's context, key questions to consider are:

- What are the characteristics of the culture and climate?
- What do teachers already know, and what do they need to know next?
- What practices are teachers currently using in the classroom? How different are current practices from desired practices?
- Does the school culture embrace new practices or resist changes?
- What are teachers' current levels of understanding of content related to state standards?
- What support do teachers need in order to implement new strategies (Killion & Roy, 2009, p. 103)?

STEP 6: PLAN INTERVENTION, IMPLEMENTATION, AND EVALUATION.

Now that the leadership team has researched interventions, team members need to adopt or adapt a professional learning program that will ensure teachers gain the necessary new knowledge and skills to improve student learning in the identified areas of need. A professional learning program is defined as "a set of purposeful, planned actions and the support system necessary to achieve the identified goals … ongoing, coherent, and linked to student achievement" (Killion, 2008, p. 11). The leadership team asks: What professional development will ensure that educators gain the necessary knowledge and skills?

The professional learning team writes a professional learning plan for the school that aligns with school and district goals, identifies student and adult learning needs, plans how to develop teachers' knowledge and skills in the specified areas of need, and outlines the means to monitor and evaluate teacher implementation and the impact on student achievement.

The leadership team now is able to answer what teachers need to know. Team members have researched successful strategies and identified, with faculty, those that they believe may help address student learning needs. Now, with the school improvement plan and district goals in front of them, they should begin to consider how teachers will learn what they need to know.

Focusing on exactly what teachers need to know and be able to do to ensure student success will guide the content and delivery of the professional learning. Content can be imparted through means from coaching to study groups. Some designs for quality school-based professional learning include action research, classroom walk-throughs, lesson study, data analysis, curriculum design, and tuning protocols. Many of these can be researched online. One source of nearly two dozen ideas is *Powerful Designs for Professional Learning,* edited by Lois Brown Easton (NSDC, 2008).

After considering various job-embedded, ongoing strategies for learning, the leadership team should commit ideas to a written plan. Schools have devised various templates for their school-based professional learning plans. Several examples appear on pp. 44-46.

Sample school-based professional development plan

District goal: Increase academic achievement for all students.

Objective 1.A: By 2012, the percentage of students who are proficient as defined by FCAT will increase for reading, and the performance gap between subgroups of students as defined by NCLB will be reduced.

1. PLANNING		2. DELIVERY AND FOLLOW-UP	
Learning needs based on data	**Resources**	**Professional development**	
Increase students' knowledge and skills for Cluster 2, especially for details/facts, main idea/essential message, and author's purpose. Decrease the number of special education and ELL students scoring below 3 on FCAT reading.	Ongoing collaboration time. Reading materials (e.g. leveled books, nonfiction). Instructional coach. Literacy coach.	*Focus* Examine content focus and alignment of assessments with language arts benchmarks. Learn and apply reading skills and strategies for Cluster 2 (main idea, plot, purpose). Examine instructional practices in relation to student outcomes through formative assessments.	*Format/type* Grade-level/ content-area meetings. Training session with follow-up in grade-level/vertical teams. Action research. Faculty meetings. Grade-level/ content-area meetings.

SMART goal (student achievement): By 2012, 75% of all students in grades 6-8 will score 3 or above on the FCAT Reading for Cluster 2 (main idea, plot, and purpose), and the weighted average performance gap will be reduced to 11.

Teacher implementation goal: All teachers will teach and monitor progress of students learning reading skills and strategies for Cluster 2 (main idea, plot, and purpose) and regularly applying the skills with different genres.

3. EVALUATION		
Teacher learning outcomes	**Teacher practice outcomes**	**Student learning outcomes**
Teachers identify reading skills and strategies at every thinking level (i.e. Bloom's Taxonomy) to engage students in becoming strategic readers. Teachers identify and explicitly teach one or more reading skills and strategies associated with different genres. Teachers will differentiate instruction to meet the needs of diverse learners. Teachers will integrate technology as a tool for differentiating instruction.	Teachers consistently model, provide opportunities for guided practice, and expect independent practice of reading skills and strategies as students work on their own.	Students develop the knowledge and skills to be able to determine the main idea/essential message in a text and identify relevant details and facts and patterns of organization as measured on the FCAT reading.

Source: Duval County (Fla.) middle school.

Sample school implementation plan

By June 2010, 80% of the students in 6th grade who were identified as at-risk on the standardized test language cluster will demonstrate growth in the attributes of good writing, including drafting, editing, and revising in all content areas as measured by a pre- and post-assessment of their written work using a locally developed rubric.

6th-grade benchmarks	Professional standards for teachers	Professional learning	Evidence of classroom application to impact teacher practice for student performance	Evidence of increase in quality of student writing
What do students need to know and be able to do?	*What do teachers need to know and be able to do to ensure student success in writing?*	*What are the possibilities for professional learning?*	*How does the teacher apply what he/she has learned in professional development to classroom practice?*	*To what extent do students apply the attributes of good writing across the content areas?*
Revise content, organization, and other aspects of writing, using self, peer, and teacher collaborative feedback (the shared response of others). Edit writing for developmentally appropriate syntax, spelling, usage, and punctuation.	As a grade-level team and as a school, we need to be able to identify attributes of good writing. We need to be able to analyze student writing data. We need to identify strategies for teaching students how to be good writers.	• Grade-level meetings. • Department meetings. • Study groups. • Collaboratively scoring student writing. • Teacher-directed (coaching, modeling). • Supervisor-directed. • District staff development courses in writing. • State convention courses.	• Student writing samples. • Scored rubrics. • Lesson plans. • Reflection. • Team minutes. • Implementation logs.	• Student writing samples (pre/post). • Standardized test.

Source: Livingston Township (N.J.) School District.

Leadership team members next review the plan, scrutinizing it from multiple perspectives. Some questions the leadership team might ask are:

- What kind of support does the program need to be successful?
- How will we support the individuals involved?
- What are we equipped to do to support and implement the professional learning, and what external resources will we need?
- What resources are we dedicating to the professional learning?
- What is our timeline for full implementation by all faculty members?
- What benchmarks along the way will help us know if we are successful?
- Are we willing to commit time, energy, and financial resources to this effort for the long term?
- How will we align this new initiative with existing efforts? What might we need to eliminate to make resources available for this program?
- How closely do the professional learning goals align with our school's improvement goals and the district's strategic goals?
- How will we assess how the program is

initiated, implemented, and sustained (Killion & Roy, 2009, p. 105)?

A logic model is a good tool to use to develop an action plan (see **Figure 3.2**). A logic model graphically represents a program's theory of change, how professional learning will result in the desired outcomes. It lays out actions and demonstrates connections. A completed logic model also is a first step toward an effective evaluation that will help determine whether the program is working.

During this planning phase, leadership team members also should simultaneously design an evaluation plan that includes formative and summative assessments. Formative evaluation is an ongoing collection of teacher implementation and student achievement data related to the professional learning target. The team should determine the measures needed during formative evaluation, how frequently the measures will be used for each data collection point, and how the team will share the results with the faculty. A summative evaluation will allow the team to determine the program's impact on student and teacher learning.

Design an evaluation of professional learning while planning the professional

Figure 3.2: Logic model

Resources	Actions	Initial outcomes (learning)	Intermediate outcomes (practice)	Intended results
Time. People. Materials. Funds.	Professional learning opportunities leading to desired outcomes for teachers and intended results for students.	Changes in knowledge and skills.	Changes in instructional practices (behaviors) and attitudes.	Increase in student achievement.

Six characteristics of professional learning that correlate with positive changes in teacher knowledge and skill are:

Focus on content:	Professional learning is directly related to the teacher's content area.
Focus on methods:	Professional learning focuses on instructional strategies.
Direction:	The more time spent on new learning, the better.
Format:	Professional learning is embedded within teachers' workday.
Collective participation:	All educators within a school participate in the same learning experiences.
Opportunities for active learning:	Professional learning includes observing in classrooms, practicing new learning, planning alone or with peers, and presenting new learning to others (NCES, 2005).

learning so that multiple sources of information will be gathered throughout the process. An effective evaluation will help guide improvement and demonstrate the impact of professional learning on teacher effectiveness and student achievement. By planning for evaluation at the same time as planning the professional learning, the team can improve program planning and be sure members will not have additional work trying to find data later — or of finding out that the data do not exist to evaluate the professional learning.

Formative/ongoing evaluation questions about the professional learning might include (Killion & Roy, 2009, p. 106):

- Is the professional learning being implemented as planned?
- Are resources adequate to implement the plan?
- To what degree are differences occurring

in implementation that may influence the program's results?

Some summative evaluation questions are:

- Has the learning achieved the intended results?
- What changes for teachers have resulted from the professional learning?
- What changes for students have resulted from the professional learning?
- What changes in the organization have resulted from the professional learning?

In addition to planning, the leadership team's role is to set expectations, support implementation, and monitor the focus of ongoing professional development. Team members are gathering data on what students are learning, what teachers are learning, and how teachers are teaching. The leadership team gathers, interprets, and shares those findings on an ongoing basis with the staff with the

Where to begin

▶ Identify a backmapping model to use in planning, and become familiar with the steps.

▶ Analyze student learning needs and school context.

▶ Review district-level data in the school improvement plan.

▶ Describe student data at the building level; attach tables and charts.

▶ Discuss data with leadership team and full faculty using **Tool 3.3**.

▶ Identify ways to best use Innovation Configuration maps with the leadership team.

▶ Develop a plan for professional learning.

▶ Outline what data to collect and create an evaluation plan at the outset.

▶ Evaluate leadership team members' leadership skills.

Reflections

• Consider the components of the backmapping model. Which of these steps are you using? How can you refine these activities to bring them in line with the model?

• Where can you find research to support the adoption of new professional learning?

• Who plans or designs professional learning for the district or school? How prepared are they to plan professional learning as described in this chapter? If they do not feel ready, who can help increase their capacity?

• How many sources of student data do you have available for analysis? How comfortable are staff in conducting their own analysis of student data? What could be done to help them become more comfortable?

• Step 6 of the backmapping process requires thoughtful planning and is typically the school's or district's first step. What are the advantages of completing steps 1 through 5 before step 6?

Source: Killion & Roy, 2009, p. 105.

Evaluation identifies school and professional learning goals and asks for:

1. Data and evidence upon which the school goal was based.

2. New knowledge, skills, and attitudes toward learning that will result from the professional learning for students, staff, and stakeholders (e.g. paraprofessionals, parents).

3. Data and evidence related to new knowledge, skills, and attitudes toward learning that show progress toward the identified school goal.

intent of adjusting the plan as needed in a cycle of continuous improvement. The ongoing cycle includes learning sessions with follow-up activities throughout the school year so that teachers are supported in transferring learning to the classroom.

STEP 7: IMPLEMENT, SUSTAIN, AND EVALUATE THE PROFESSIONAL LEARNING INTERVENTION.

In many schools, new initiatives are quick to die after an initial burst of enthusiasm. Not all staff may be committed to the change, and the early adopters sometimes move on to try something else. New initiatives succeed only with careful nurturing.

Together, grade-level or department learning teams and the school leadership team monitor how teachers are implementing the professional learning by regularly examining

teachers' practice and student achievement data. The leadership team should keep in mind the definition of high-quality professional learning at all times, and continually refocus and adjust plans to meet the definition as plans progress. Leadership team members are responsible for guiding colleagues to meet high standards for professional learning and teaching practices. The Innovation Configuration maps in Appendix B can help in recalibrating. Revisit the maps for selected standards regularly to evaluate progress toward the ideal levels and review expectations.

To sustain a focus on results, monitoring should continue over several years. School leaders will need to plan and commit necessary resources to guide a cycle of continuous improvement.

Chapter 5 provides more depth about evaluating professional learning.

Additional resources

O'Neill, J. & Conzemius, A. (2006). *The power of SMART goals: Using goals to improve student learning.* Bloomington, IN: Solution Tree.

Wisconsin Information Network for Successful Schools. (n.d.). *Tips for using the School Improvement Planning Tool.* Available at http://goal.learningpt.org/winss/sip/tips.htm.

Tools index

TOOL	TITLE	USE
3.1	Using the Innovation Configuration maps	**Tool 3.1** describes how to use an IC map to determine current status of desired outcomes and use of levels to identify next steps in making progress toward the ideal levels.
3.2	Backmapping models	**Tool 3.2** provides examples of backmapping models from one state (Iowa) and one district (Green Bay Area Public Schools) for schools to follow in a cycle of continuous improvement.
3.3	Response sheet for discussing school data	**Tool 3.3** is a response sheet for a leadership team to use to structure discussions about school data.
3.4	Planning chart for action ideas	**Tool 3.4** is a template for the leadership team to use in planning action steps based on adult and student learning needs.
3.5	Best practices for professional learning	**Tool 3.5** is a chart to guide the school leadership team in identifying current practices aligned with identified principles and to help the team reach consensus on adopting or adapting the principles for professional learning opportunities at the school.
3.6	Journal/research reflection sheet	**Tool 3.6** is a sample template for recording and sharing information from professional reading.
3.7	Reading educational research	**Tool 3.7** is a set of questions to guide the leadership team when reading educational research aligned with student needs to help team members make decisions for professional learning.

Tools index

TOOL	TITLE	USE
3.8	Fishbone diagram	**Tool 3.8** will assist the leadership team in taking results from data analysis and identifying root causes of the identified problems.
3.9	Critical inquiry process	**Tool 3.9** is a process that the leadership team can use to structure a discussion around a problem. The process includes five questions that might require a series of meetings to discuss.
3.10	Gap analysis	**Tool 3.10** is a procedure to help the leadership team determine needs and identify problems before action planning.
3.11	KASAB chart	**Tool 3.11** is a template for identifying the knowledge, attitudes, skills, aspirations, and behaviors (KASAB) for students, teachers, administrators, and parents related to targeted areas of need.
3.12	Lesson study	**Tool 3.12** is an article that describes the steps of the lesson study cycle and tools for preparing, observing, and debriefing a study lesson to learn more about how to improve instruction.
3.13	Snapshots of learning	**Tool 3.13** is an article that describes how to use classroom walk-throughs as a way to capture what practices are being implemented in classrooms as a result of the professional learning.
3.14	Teacher research leads to learning, action	**Tool 3.14** is an article that describes the steps for conducting action research with tools to help staff use action research as a professional learning design.

Tools index

TOOL	TITLE	USE
3.15	Group wise: Strategies for examining student work together	**Tool 3.15** is an article that provides strategies for staff to use to examine student work collaboratively to learn more about their teaching practices.
3.16	Process: Select the strategy that works for your context and content	**Tool 3.16** is an article to assist the leadership team in learning how to select strategies for professional learning aligned with a specific context and content.
3.17	Work smarter, not harder: SMART goals keep key objectives in focus	**Tool 3.17** is an article that describes the SMART goal process, with sample tree diagrams showing climate and writing goals. The article outlines five meetings for teams to use in developing SMART goals.
3.18	What's your professional development IQ?	**Tool 3.18** is an article and tool to engage different stakeholders in conversation about what they know about teaching and professional learning.
3.19	Decisive action: Crucial steps streamline decision-making process	**Tool 3.19** is an article that provides tools for decision making, such as list reduction, nominal group process, criteria sorting, weighted voting, and paired comparisons.
3.20	Transform your group into a team	**Tool 3.20** is an article that provides information about the four stages of team development (forming, storming, norming, and performing) and a questionnaire for a team to use to determine its current stage.
3.21	Powerful conversations	**Tool 3.21** is an article that provides directions and a script to help team members engage in role playing how to have powerful conversations at their school.

Tools index

TOOL	TITLE	USE
3.22	Listen carefully: Good communication skills build relationships that foster school improvement	**Tool 3.22** is an article about the importance of having good communication skills in order to build relationships. Tools are provided to assist the leadership team and staff in improving their communication skills.
3.23	Meeting expectations: Turn staff gatherings into learning opportunities	**Tool 3.23** is an article that describes how a leadership team can plan effective staff meetings using collaborative tools for professional learning aligned with student and adult learning needs.
3.24	Educator, know thyself: Learning where you are is the first step in establishing your direction	**Tool 3.24** provides tools (school culture survey, parent/community involvement assessment) for the leadership team to use to determine current reality. A tool, Rate Yourself as a Team Player, will help team members assess their behavior within the leadership team or learning teams at the school.
3.25	Support system: School improvement plans work best when staff learning is included	**Tool 3.25** is an article about school improvement plans. It provides a list of questions for the leadership team to ask as they are planning and tools to assist the leadership team in the planning process.
3.26	The numbers game: Measure progress by analyzing data	**Tool 3.26** is an article that describes the steps for measuring progress by analyzing data and provides tools to assist the leadership team in monitoring progress using data.
3.27	Smart moves: Achieving your vision depends on follow-through	**Tool 3.27** is an article that describes the need for 30-, 60-, and 90-day action plans to ensure follow-through with professional learning and ongoing data gathering to inform practice.

Tools index

TOOL	TITLE	USE
3.28	School improvement plan: Template for professional development	**Tool 3.28** provides a sample of a professional development plan as part of the school improvement plan.
3.29	Sample school-based professional development plan template	**Tool 3.29** is an example of a school-based professional development plan focused on aligning professional learning with student and teacher outcomes and on gathering evidence of implementation and results.

"Teacher learning communities build a faculty's collective capacity to provide high-quality, rigorous instruction to all students and so enhance capability to respond quickly and effectively to evidence of failure and surprises."

— Milbrey McLaughlin and Joan Talbert, *Building School-Based Teacher Learning Communities*, 2006, p. 6

Chapter 4

SUPPORTING
school-based professional learning

Leadership teams help sustain and support colleagues through a process of improvement that will challenge the status quo and move people outside of their comfort zones. Leadership team members are responsible for creating the structures and processes for collaborative work that promotes collegiality and shared responsibility. As Richard Elmore states (2002), "Leaders engage people in shaping the content and conditions of their own learning in organizationally coherent ways."

Team members work collaboratively with teachers across the school to establish structures (team membership, norms, team leaders, times to meet, etc.) and processes (protocols, norms, reporting mechanisms, etc.) for ongoing learning teams focused on improving instructional practice and student achievement, help teachers work collaboratively in different teams (grade-level, department, course, interdisciplinary, whole school, etc.), and support all teachers in taking responsibility for the success of all students.

Learning teams are increasingly the structure for much of teachers' professional learning time. According to Milbrey McLaughlin and Joan Talbert (2006, p. 7), "Shared vision, collaboration, and learning together provide the foundation for teachers to take collective responsibility for students' success; the community's interdependent work structure allows for teachers to act on this vision. An established teacher learning community makes the school accountable for student learning rather than locating accountability exclusively in an external mechanism, such as the high-stakes testing systems used in many areas."

Characteristics of an ongoing team

Anne Conzemius and Jan O'Neill (2002, p. 24) have identified the following characteristics of an ongoing team:

- Exists for the duration of an initiative;
- Has a relatively stable membership that rotates based on a long-range plan;
- Is focused on a broad, ongoing mission;
- Includes members with a similar perspective or functions; and
- Develops members' strong allegiance to the team.

Elmore notes that "the complex nature of instructional practice requires people to operate in networks of shared and complementary expertise rather than in hierarchies." Collaboration among school staff can occur in a variety of ways, including grade-level/department teams, vertical teams, content areas, whole faculty groups, or collaborative learning teams. The configuration of the team depends on its purpose.

FINDING TIME

Although the teams may meet in different configurations, the school leadership team needs to understand the research related to the amount of time teachers need to meet in order to change instructional practices and impact student achievement. In a review of more than 1,300 studies about professional development, researchers found that teachers who spent 49 hours on a single focus raised student achievement by about 21 percentile points (Yoon, Duncan, Lee, Scarloss, & Shapley, 2007, p. iii). The leadership team should advocate for adequate time and arrange for job-embedded learning.

Many educators are uncertain how to find time for any additional tasks during the workday, given the sometimes seemingly overwhelming tasks they already face. By restructuring the way they use time, however, teachers can refresh themselves through collegial professional time and benefit students. **Tools 4.2** and **4.11** provide ideas on finding time.

Dennis Sparks wrote (1999), "When meetings and staff development days have a laser-like focus on student learning, and when teachers see the benefits of their learning in their own classrooms, they will actively seek ways to increase the amount of time available for collaborative work rather than resist it as a distraction and intrusion on their already full professional lives. Thus motivated, they will invent ways that fit their unique circumstances to have more time during their workdays and throughout the year."

NSDC advocates for most professional learning to occur at the school level. Ideally, each school can arrange its time and other resources so that 25% of the work week and 10% of the budget are allocated for teachers' professional learning.

The leadership team is responsible for ensuring that teachers use collaborative time set aside for professional learning wisely. Doing what was done in the past during collaboration time will not improve results. This time should be used to focus on learning goals outlined in the leadership team's professional learning plan and to implement strategies and processes the leadership team has identified and worked with staff to create.

The leadership team serves to educate teachers and others responsible for allocating time about the amount of time needed, to seek creative ways to carve out learning time, and to work with teachers to manage and use the time to support the learning plan.

TRANSFERRING KNOWLEDGE

As teachers gain new knowledge and skills in their professional learning teams, it is important for the school leadership team to remember the components of effective learning: presentation of theory, demonstration, practice and feedback, and peer coaching.

- **Theory:** The content is explained (e.g. what it is, why it is important, and how to teach it).
- **Demonstration:** Instructional practices are modeled.
- **Practice:** Teachers implement instructional practices during the professional development session.
- **Coaching:** Teachers receive ongoing support and guidance when practicing new

strategies in their own classrooms.

The leadership team should incorporate this knowledge into work with learning teams and teachers in using their professional learning time. **Table 4.1** shows the level of teachers' transfer of their learning to classroom practice based on an effective method.

PROVIDING INCENTIVES

As learning continues, supporting colleagues may mean leadership team members visit learning teams regularly, helping teachers troubleshoot and paying close attention to building a culture of continuous improvement focused on student learning goals.

One way to create a supportive school environment is to create professional incentives, according to Anne Jolly (2008, p. 86). Jolly says incentives may be to:

- *Connect professional learning team work with other school programs and initiatives.* Teams' work should align with the school improvement plan as well as the school leadership team's professional learning plan.

Table 4.1: Professional development outcomes

Professional development elements	Knowledge level *Estimated percentage of understanding of the content*	Skill attainment *Estimated percentage of teachers demonstrating proficiency in the instructional practice*	Transfer to practice *Estimated percentage of teachers regularly implementing instructional practices in the classroom*
Theory	10%	5%	0%
Demonstrations	30%	20%	0%
Practice	60%	60%	5%
Coaching	95%	95%	95%

Source: Joyce & Showers, 2002, p. 78.

Aligning work helps keep teachers from feeling overburdened.

- *Offer education credit for professional learning.* The leadership team can explore an arrangement with a local college or university to offer credit that allows teachers to meet recertification requirements. The leadership team can support teachers by helping them develop templates for team logs, plans, and portfolios that would meet continuing education requirements.
- *Regularly showcase teams' work.* Ask the principal for time during a staff meeting to highlight learning teams' work, or find ways to let all the staff know about each team's progress through workroom information displays or other sharing.
- *Give team members opportunities and training on using technology to communicate and promote their work.* Help teachers learn to use e-mail, electronic logs, and other means to post announcements, share information, and gain feedback.
- *Create an identity.* Teams can develop their own name, motto, and logo to help members identify with the group and to rally spirit.

It is up to leadership team members to work with the administration to facilitate ways to help teachers sustain the momentum. Incentives are key to maintaining energy throughout the time it takes to see an initiative through.

STAGES OF CONCERN

Through the process of reforming the way teachers and students process learning, the leadership team must also focus on personal needs. Learning brings change. Supporting

---

Incentives for teachers

The proper incentives communicate what the organization values and further teachers' professional growth. Consider these ideas:

- Memberships in professional organizations.
- Subscriptions to education journals.
- Time and registration fees for a conference.
- Public celebrations of team achievements.
- A voice in decisions about professional learning teams.
- Time to visit other classrooms or schools.
- Resources and materials.
- Access to a consultant or coach.
- Business cards.
- Specific acknowledgment within the school and community of the quality and outcomes of work.

Source: Jolly, 2008, p. 35.

RESPONSES TO CHANGE

Shirley Hord et al. (1998) identified various ways individuals respond to change. In any group, members likely fall into these categories:

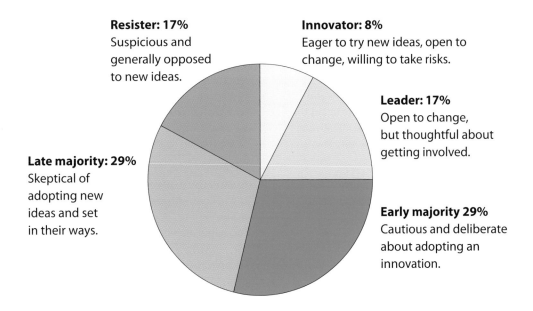

Resister: 17%
Suspicious and generally opposed to new ideas.

Innovator: 8%
Eager to try new ideas, open to change, willing to take risks.

Leader: 17%
Open to change, but thoughtful about getting involved.

Late majority: 29%
Skeptical of adopting new ideas and set in their ways.

Early majority 29%
Cautious and deliberate about adopting an innovation.

colleagues in times of learning is critical for learning to take root. The Concerns-Based Adoption Model, developed by the Southwest Educational Development Laboratory, anticipates individuals' reactions to change, the stages they are likely to experience, and the types of questions they may ask.

For many people, the first response to change is to try to understand the information and to ask, "How will this affect me?" Next, they may move to trying to understand how to apply the new knowledge: "How do I do this?" When those questions are resolved, they are ready to focus on how the learning may affect students and to assess its impact. Stages of Concern, one of the tools from this model, outlines seven stages individuals may experience during change and ways to assess individuals' readiness to progress. For leadership team members, understanding these stages is essential. Before working with teachers on how

to change practices to meet the identified school learning goal, team members will have to address teachers' comfort level with the change itself and pay attention over time to teachers' concerns in various stages. This diagnostic tool suggests that any change initiative may take several years before concerns are resolved and teachers are able to move new practices into implementation. Once teachers are implementing the change in their classrooms, another tool, Levels of Use, can help the leadership team identify specific levels of implementation based on teaching behaviors.

EXAMINING THE WALLPAPER

The leadership team can be a primary influence on the success of learning teams, fostering commitment to group work and supporting teams through the process of change. As peers, leadership team members can exert great influence on teacher collaboration and assist in creating a unified purpose among staff.

STAGE OF CONCERN	HOW TEAM MEMBERS FEEL AND THINK AT EACH LEVEL	EXAMPLES OF INTERVENTIONS
AWARENESS	I have little information, concern, or involvement with professional learning teams. I am not concerned about this change and am not doing anything about it.	• Web resources and written resources about professional learning teams. • Opportunities to attend workshops and conferences. • Conversations providing a rationale for professional learning teams.
INFORMATIONAL	I have a general interest in professional learning teams and would like to know more about this process. I'm taking the initiative to learn more about learning teams.	• Question-and-answer sessions. • Discussions with individuals who have expertise with professional learning teams via conferences or webinars. • Opportunities to attend workshops and conferences.
PERSONAL	I want to know the personal impact of the professional learning team initiative.	• Information about time and work commitments. • Involvement in planning for learning teams. • Discussions with experts in professional learning teams. • Facilitated discussions.
MANAGEMENT	I am concerned about how professional learning teams will be managed in practice and what members need to know in order to do this work.	• Organizing and planning sessions. • Information on logistics and debriefings. • Involvement in planning for professional learning teams. • Training in learning team work.
CONSEQUENCE	I want to know how my work in a professional learning team affects my colleagues and my students, and how to make my involvement have more impact. I am moving from simply attending meetings to making changes to improve teaching and learning.	• Surveys. • Self-assessments. • Reflection. • Experimentation. • Communication with other learning teams. • Assistance with diagnostic activities such as looking at student work. • Access to research and study materials.
COLLABORATION	I share, coordinate, and align my professional growth and teaching practices with others on my team. I depend on them, and I give them help and support. I have joined forces with other teachers to have a collective impact on teaching and learning.	• More frequent opportunities to share, coordinate, and learn with colleagues. • Opportunities to observe colleagues. • Schoolwide information sharing about learning teams. • Communication and interaction with other professional learning teams. • Opportunities to share at conferences.
REFOCUSING	I am interested in making our professional learning team even more effective, and I have ideas about modifications that might work even better.	• Review of research on professional learning teams. • Field-testing of products from professional learning team work. • Data analysis. • Consistent and regular support.

Source: Jolly, 2008; Hall & Hord, 2005.

LEVELS OF USE	WHAT TEAM MEMBERS DO AT EACH LEVEL	EXAMPLES OF INTERVENTIONS
Nonuse	Team members demonstrate no interest, no involvement, or are taking no action.	• Written information and web resources. • Overviews and displays. • Explanation of the rationale for professional learning teams. • Personal contacts with knowledgeable users.
Orientation	Team members express a general interest in professional learning teams, would like to know more, and are taking the initiative to learn more about the professional learning team process.	• Workshops. • Question-and-answer sessions. • Discussions with facilitators. • Talks with experienced team members.
Preparation	Team members are making definite plans to begin participating in professional learning teams and are learning the processes and skills needed to successfully implement this initiative.	• Guided overview of tools and materials. • Advice and tools for learning team management. • Modeling and practice with teaming strategies. • Consensus on area for team focus.
Mechanical	Team members are attempting to organize and master the tasks required in the early stages of implementation. The focus is mainly on day-to-day use of learning teams with little reflection.	• Study and research to deepen content knowledge in a focus area. • Use of norms to smooth bumps. • Regular self-assessments by team members of their teamwork. • Logistical help and support.
Routine	Team members are making few or no changes and have an established, comfortable pattern of working in a professional learning team. Little preparation or thought is being given to improving the use of learning teams.	• Study and research to deepen content knowledge in the focus area. • Application of learning to the classroom. • Examination of student work. • Development and use of formative assessments.
Refinement	Team members are making changes to increase the impact and consequences of professional learning teams.	• Study and research to deepen content knowledge in the focus area. • Development and use of joint instructional strategies. • Observations of colleagues who are using strategies. • Examination of student work. • Use of formative assessments.
Integration	Team members are working deliberately to coordinate and combine efforts with others using professional learning teams in order to have a collective impact.	• Professional learning team activities and information shared schoolwide. • Learning teams used as a vehicle for collaborative mentoring. • Work with colleagues to develop joint instructional practices.
Renewal	Team members reevaluate professional learning teams and seek ways to make them increasingly effective in order to achieve greater impact.	• Data analysis. • Review of new information and research. • Field testing of new instructional products. • Consistent and regular support.

Source: Jolly, 2008; Hall & Hord, 2005.

DESIRED OUTCOMES

The leadership team should align the school-based professional learning with NSDC's Standards for Staff Development. The following desired outcomes for the leadership team are identified on the Innovation Configuration map for NSDC's Design standard for leadership teams, which should help guide leadership team members in their work with teachers using different designs for professional learning aligned with the context and content (Killion & Harrison, 2006, pp. 183-186).

These outcomes describe the ideal level on the IC map for leadership teams.

Desired outcome: The leadership team designs and facilitates a variety of in-depth, sustained professional learning experiences aligned with the school improvement goals for student achievement.	▶ Designs and facilitates a variety of in-depth, sustained, and collaborative professional learning (e.g. lesson study, peer coaching, examining student work, study groups, writing and scoring common assessments, joint instructional planning, etc.) that aligns with school improvement goals for student achievement, that works as a coherent whole, and that places responsibility primarily on participants in their learning.
	▶ Connects the work of collaborative teams and the larger goal of improving student learning.
	▶ Designs learning strategies based on clearly stated outcomes for teacher and student learning.
	▶ Collects and uses data from teacher concern and prior knowledge surveys, classroom observations, informal conversations with teachers, and current schoolwide student data to design professional learning opportunities for deepening content knowledge and refining instructional practices.
Desired outcome: The leadership team supports implementation of new and/or refined instructional practices that result from in-depth, sustained professional learning.	▶ Works with principal and teachers to create tools, such as checklists, Innovation Configuration maps, rubrics, etc., to describe and support implementation of new and/or refined instructional practices.
	▶ Facilitates daily conversations within and among learning teams about teaching and learning.
	▶ Sustains conversations over time to examine continuous improvement.
	▶ Provides concrete examples of successful implementation.
	▶ Helps teachers access resources to support implementation.
	▶ Facilitates problem solving to overcome barriers associated with implementation.

DESIRED OUTCOMES

The leadership team should align the school-based professional learning with NSDC's Standards for Staff Development. The following desired outcomes for the leadership team are identified on the Innovation Configuration map for NSDC's Design standard for leadership teams, which should help guide leadership team members in their work with teachers using different designs for professional learning aligned with the context and content (Killion & Harrison, 2006, pp. 183-186).

These outcomes describe the ideal level on the IC map for leadership teams.

Desired outcome: The leadership team provides classroom-based support for implementation of new and/or refined instructional practices.	▶ Selects classroom-based support that aligns with teachers' level of comfort and expertise (e.g. years of experience, current knowledge and skills, etc.).
	▶ Provides demonstration, co-teaching, and observation and feedback to support implementation of new and/or refined instructional practices.
	▶ Designs and supports multiple classroom experiences that deepen understanding and meaning of new concepts and strategies.
	▶ Engages teachers in conducting peer coaching or walk-throughs to see examples of implementation.
	▶ Facilitates teachers to problem solve and adapt new strategies to match classroom and individual student learning needs, content, and other circumstances.
	▶ Seeks teacher feedback to improve coaching skills and practices.
Desired outcome: The leadership team engages teachers in reflection to refine and integrate effective classroom practice.	▶ Engages teachers in reflective teaching and learning conversations using a variety of tools.
	▶ Supports teachers as they reflect on previously taught lessons for the purpose of improving or refining instruction.

Team members are responsible for what Elmore describes as "examining the wallpaper." He writes (2002), "People who work in schools do not pay attention to the connection between how they organize and manage themselves and how they take care of their own and their students' learning. The structure and resources of the organization are like wallpaper — after living with the same wallpaper for a certain number of years, people cease to see it."

Leaders have a key role in helping colleagues become more aware of the connection between professional learning and student learning and reminding peers that well-designed and implemented professional learning is a long-term investment in themselves as teachers and in children's ability to achieve their potential.

Where to begin

▶ Identify needed supports within the school. Determine how learning teams may be configured to best work toward achieving the learning goal.

▶ Examine ways to create time for learning teams and advocate for job-embedded learning time.

▶ Understand the tenets of effective learning and work with teams to structure time so that learning transfers into practice.

▶ Understand how individuals respond to change.

▶ Work to provide incentives to maintain momentum.

▶ Examine the school "wallpaper." Carefully review school structures and resources to be able to suggest whether efforts are congruent with achieving the identified learning goal.

Additional resources

Jolly, A. (2008). *Team to teach*. Oxford, OH: NSDC.

Von Frank, V. (Ed.) (2006). *Finding time for professional learning*. Oxford, OH: NSDC.

Tools index

TOOL	TITLE	USE
4.1	Focused, job-embedded learning leads to quality teaching	**Tool 4.1** is an article that describes the importance of developing a system of professional learning based on NSDC's definition to make team learning meaningful in improving teaching practices and student performance.
4.2	Think outside the clock: Create time for professional learning	**Tool 4.2** is an article that describes different ways for a school to find time for professional learning and provides examples of how some schools have found time.
4.3	Build a bridge between workshop and classroom	**Tool 4.3** is an article that describes the importance of follow-up activities to ensure that teachers put their training into practice. Some tools are provided to assist in transferring training to classrooms.
4.4	Making the most of professional learning communities	**Tool 4.4** is an article that describes three recommended roles for members of professional learning communities: critical friend, analyst of student work, and continuous learner.
4.5	With the right strategies, data analysis bears fruit	**Tool 4.5** is an article that describes the need to select the right strategies-based data and focus resources on high priorities. A classroom observation protocol is provided as a tool to help the leadership team collect information about teaching practices.
4.6	Innovation Configurations light the way for deeper learning	**Tool 4.6** provides a protocol for developing a shared vision to implement NSDC's Standards for Staff Development using Innovation Configuration maps for different role groups, such as teacher, school-based staff developer, and principal.

Tools index

TOOL	TITLE	USE
4.7	Collaboration is the key to unlocking potential	**Tool 4.7** is an article that focuses on creating a culture of collaboration and building teacher leadership.
4.8	A collegial conversation: Talking about instruction helps teachers find new ways to engage	**Tool 4.8** is an article that describes steps teachers can engage in to have collegial conversations about instruction to find new ways to engage students.
4.9	Boost the learning power of school-based staff: Innovation Configuration maps guide the way	**Tool 4.9** is an article that describes how Innovation Configuration maps can be used to establish a clear vision of NSDC's standards in action, assess implementation of the standards, and set goals for improving school-based professional development.
4.10	Selecting coaches	**Tool 4.10** is an article that describes the difference between school-based and district-based coaches and the importance of the selection process in ensuring coaching improves teaching practices and student achievement.
4.11	Strategies for finding time	**Tool 4.11** is an article that describes the need to find time during the school day for all educators to engage in quality professional learning to gain new knowledge and skills based on student needs.
4.12	Protocols: A facilitator's best friend	**Tool 4.12** is an article that describes the basics of using protocols to guide teachers in professional conversation and provides three protocols (Wagon Wheel, Three Levels of Text, Success Analysis Protocol).
4.13	Feedback analysis	**Tool 4.13** guides team members in expressing the quality and usefulness of feedback received. A checklist describes what feedback should look and sound like.

Tools index

TOOL	TITLE	USE
4.14	Team progress reminders	**Tool 4.14** will help the leadership team monitor team progress.
4.15	A measure of concern: Research-based program aids innovation by addressing teacher concerns	**Tool 4.15** provides the leadership team with a description of how to measure change using Stages of Concern, one of three tools from the Concerns-Based Adoption Model (CBAM). This article will help the leadership team gather data from teachers by asking questions or using a questionnaire. Use the results to address common concerns about change when planning professional learning at the school.
4.16	Navigate the fluctuating undercurrents of change	**Tool 4.16** describes how a leadership team can use Stages of Concern to identify teachers' feelings as they implement new practices. The information will help team members understand NSDC's Learning standard, which focuses on applying knowledge about adult learning and change.
4.17	What concerns do you have?	**Tool 4.17** describes three ways the leadership team can assess staff feelings and concerns, use that information to support teachers implementing new practices, and learn appropriate interventions based on identified Stages of Concern.
4.18	Many schools, one complex measure: St. Louis district synthesizes the lessons of reform	**Tool 4.18** provides information on how an urban district used the Stages of Concern questionnaire to track teachers' perceptions of participation in professional development and implementation of instructional models. The leadership team can use this information to consider how it might use the Stages of Concern questionnaire to track changes at the school level.

"Evaluation — not just data — is increasingly important for reforming schools. Evaluation provides a way for school and district leaders to answer questions about the impact of their work. Evaluation provides insight into what is working and what is not. Evaluation can provide information for making decisions about policy and practice."

— Joellen Killion, *Assessing Impact: Evaluating Staff Development,* 2nd edition, 2008

Chapter 5

EVALUATING
the impact

The idea of evaluation connects with educators in different ways. Almost everyone associates evaluation directly with student achievement or job performance. When thinking about evaluating professional development, we might vaguely recall a simple survey completed at the end of a traditional workshop that asked basic questions focused on participants' satisfaction, such as, "Was the presenter knowledgeable and well organized?" "Was the room comfortable?" "Was this session helpful?"

Today, however, educators are asked to show evidence of professional learning's impact on instructional practices and, preferably, on improving student performance. To be able to do that, evaluation must be a component of every professional learning plan.

Conducting a more in-depth evaluation, such as an impact evaluation, can be daunting, conjuring memories of college courses in statistics and raising fears about the need to use mathematical formulas and statistical analyses. Evaluations need not be that complex.

The evaluation plan needs to include initial changes expected in teachers' knowledge and skills, intermediate behavioral changes, and the intended student achievement level. Identifying changes and results helps guide the team's plan for professional learning, as well as selection of the best tools and instruments to monitor progress toward the identified changes.

By developing the evaluation plan simultaneously with the school professional learning plan, the leadership team can be selective about resources and activities that fit with its goals. Identifying the tools and instruments early, such as surveys, teacher artifacts, or student work, also will help participating teachers be clear about what data to collect over time and will make clear the expectations for classroom implementation and accountability.

Creating an evaluation plan at the start of planning professional development also helps the team ensure that the learning design, content, and duration align with the team's stated goals. The evaluation will help the leadership team determine whether the professional learning plan is solid by enabling the team to connect the plan with clearly stated outcomes related to teaching and student learning; helping members improve the plan as it is under way and as the team reviews and interprets data about how teachers' learning and implementation is progressing; and helping document the effect of professional development on student achievement. Only by evaluating the effectiveness of the effort can the team adjust plans midcourse to maximize teachers' learning so that student achievement is impacted. Monitoring progress toward the identified goals and making adjustments as needed are valuable both internally and to outside stakeholders.

Joellen Killion (2008) states, "To evaluate a staff development program's impact on student achievement, the measure of achievement must be aligned with all of the following: the curriculum content, the pedagogy (instructional practice), the assessment tool, the instructional resources students use in their classrooms, and the content of the educators' staff development program" (p. 29). Killion (2003) has outlined an eight-step process for evaluations. **Figure 5.1** summarizes this process. The steps fall into three sections: planning, conducting, and reporting.

PLANNING

An evaluation begun simultaneously with the plan for professional learning will help ensure that educators' professional learning improves student achievement. Careful evaluation planning can highlight problems or issues with the learning plan design, content, or duration. Killion separates planning into three steps.

Assess evaluability. The first step in evaluation planning is to determine whether the professional learning program is ready for evaluation. Killion (2008) states that a professional learning program is ready for an evaluation if "it clearly articulates what will occur, the actions within the plan are sufficient to produce the results expected, and there is a clear understanding of what changes will lead to the intended results" (2008, p. 31).

Evaluation planners ask:
- Is the professional learning conceptually and logically feasible? In other words, does it seem likely that it has potential to produce the results it intends?
- Are the goals, objectives, activities, resources, initial or intermediate outcomes, and intended results clearly stated and understood by key stakeholders?
- Is this evaluation worth doing? (Killion, 2008, p. 31).

If the answer to all these questions is affirmative, an evaluation is worthwhile. If not, the team may work more on the learning plan to ensure its content, design, and duration align with the school's identified goals. By considering an evaluation during planning, the team improves its planning and the likelihood of a valuable outcome for the effort.

Formulate evaluation questions. An evaluation might be formative, summative, or both. The team might look at its action plan, the logic model, and its road map of action steps, or theory of change, to generate formative evaluation questions. Formative questions are developed based on the expected changes in teachers' knowledge, skills, and behavior. For example, "To what extent are teachers implementing the (name of initiative)?" "What facilitated or impeded implementation in the classroom?" Summative evaluation questions are based on the stated student achievement goals or the degree to which the program achieved its results. For example, "Did student achievement increase?"

The questions will help guide what evidence the team should collect to be able to demonstrate the link between professional learning and changes in instructional practices that lead to increased student achievement. They also will help the team think about who will need the information, which can help guide and determine the evaluation content and the questions themselves.

For example, the school board will have different needs than the school leadership team. Board members might want to know only about improvements in student achievement, while the school leadership team might want to know how the school-based professional learning changed instructional practices.

Evaluation questions to think about:

1. What changes have occurred in teachers' practices as a result of the school-based professional learning?

2. What components of the professional learning have been most influential in affecting changes in instructional practices?

3. How has professional development affected student achievement?

Construct an evaluation framework. The framework is the evaluation plan. The framework establishes what data team members will collect,

outlines a time frame, and details how members will analyze data. Outlining these pieces early helps team members make sure adequate data is available to draw conclusions and avoids having team members try to go back and reconstruct information — or finding that appropriate supporting data simply is not available.

As the team plans the evaluation, one useful guide to consider is Thomas Guskey's five levels for evaluating professional development (Guskey, 2001). These five levels include:

- Level 1: Participants' reaction.
- Level 2: Participants' learning.
- Level 3: Organizational support and change.
- Level 4: Participants' use of new knowledge and skills.
- Level 5: Student learning outcomes.

Tool 5.10 provides additional information about Guskey's levels.

CONDUCTING

The process and results of the evaluation will be only as good as the data the team collects. During this critical phase, team members must carefully follow systematic, scientific processes to be sure the data are reliable. Team members may need some training to be consistent in their methods for collecting data and may need additional knowledge to learn to analyze and interpret the information they collect.

Two books to help in this work are *Assessing Impact: Evaluating Staff Development,* 2nd ed., by Joellen Killion (Corwin Press with NSDC, 2008) and *Evaluating Professional Development,* by Thomas Guskey (Corwin Press, 2001).

Before collecting data, team members need to develop a protocol for how to do so. If data are being collected using a tool the team has developed, pilot the tool to determine whether the instrument is clear to users and whether the information collected meets the intent. Assess the validity of the instrument and refine the process.

Figure 5.1: 8-step process of evaluation

An effective evaluation of a professional learning program follows an eight-step process:

Planning phase

1. **Assess** evaluability: Determine whether the staff development program is ready to be evaluated.

2. **Formulate** evaluation questions: Design formative and summative evaluation questions.

3. **Construct** evaluation framework: Determine the evidence needed to answer the evaluation questions, data sources, data collection methodology, logistics of data collection, and data analysis methods.

Conducting phase

4. **Collect** data: Manage data collection process and collected data.

5. **Organize** and analyze data: Organize, analyze, and display data.

6. **Interpret** data: Interpret data to determine merit, worth, and/or impact and to make recommendations for improvement.

Reporting phase

7. **Disseminate** findings: Identify audiences to receive findings, the most appropriate format for communicating findings to each, and disseminate findings.

8. **Evaluate** the evaluation: Reflect on the evaluation process, the knowledge and skills of the evaluation team, the resources and methodologies used, and the findings to improve future evaluations.

Source: Killion, 2003, p. 14.

The American Evaluation Association and the Joint Committee on Standards for Educational Evaluation offer standards and guidelines for data collection. See the resources listed at the end of this chapter for how to access this information.

Collect data. Team members will need to follow the same protocol for collecting data so that the information is consistent and accurate. Collect data on an ongoing basis throughout professional learning to be able to measure changes and determine whether benchmarks are achieved. Use multiple sources of data to provide cross-checks, along with a system of checks and balances to ensure data are recorded accurately.

Organize and analyze data. This may not be a complex statistical analysis. Many evaluations can be done by considering both qualitative (anecdotal) and quantitative (mathematical) data, such as using a coding system to identify emerging patterns, averages, medians, modes, and historical trends. Refer

Figure 5.2: Conceptual framework for studying the effects of professional learning

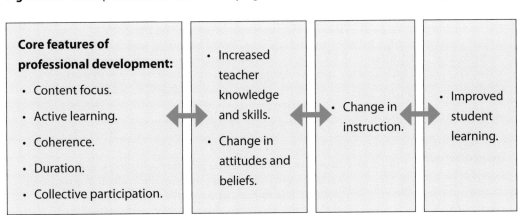

Core features of professional development:

- Content focus.
- Active learning.
- Coherence.
- Duration.
- Collective participation.

- Increased teacher knowledge and skills.
- Change in attitudes and beliefs.

- Change in instruction.

- Improved student learning.

Source: Desimone, 2009.

to the initial evaluation question to determine how to best view the data. Identify patterns and look for outliers. Develop charts and graphs to display findings.

Interpret data. Understanding what the data reveal is essential to taking the next step toward improvement. If a trend shows an increase or decrease, the next question is "Why?" For example, if student data show a trend of improving 4th-grade reading scores, can the team find improvement in specific areas of student scores, such as reading comprehension, that align with changes in instructional practices that relate to the content of the school-based professional learning, such as a focus on strategies for teaching reading comprehension? If data reveal a sudden dip in 3rd-grade math, was there a change in faculty? Group perspective and analysis are key, and the team may even consider involving other stakeholders to gain additional views.

The team will reach conclusions about whether the professional learning occurred as planned, whether it was worthwhile and achieved its intended goals, and, depending on the type of evaluation, how participants perceived its value.

Killion (2003, p. 21) cautions, "Claims of contribution, those stating that the program

influenced student achievement, are made when the evaluation design is descriptive or quasi-experimental. Claims of attribution, that staff development and nothing else caused the results, require experimental, randomized design not often used in evaluation studies."

REPORTING

As tempting as it may be to rest on the results, reporting out is a crucial piece of the evaluation and of professional learning. Having invested in the evaluation process and spent considerable time collecting and evaluating data, teams can't stop before communicating the results with key stakeholders. The work now is developing the means of communicating, and this effort, too, can offer new opportunities for leadership through developing and presenting reports.

Disseminate findings. Prepare written and oral reports of the results, basing the format on the audience(s) identified when the evaluation questions were written. Determine how much information and how much depth each audience may need, in addition to the best format in which to present it. Written reports might range from a summary, a longer paper with technical findings, or a newsletter article to a simple

DESIRED OUTCOMES

The leadership team should align the school-based professional learning with NSDC's Standards for Staff Development. The following desired outcomes for the leadership team are identified on the Innovation Configuration map for NSDC's Evaluation standard and describe how the principal and teacher leaders work together to monitor implementation of the learning plan so teachers continuously improve their practices to increase student achievement (NSDC, 2003, pp. 78-79).

These outcomes describe the ideal level on the IC map for leadership teams.

Desired outcome: Develops a comprehensive plan for conducting ongoing evaluation of staff development programs.	▶ Develops a comprehensive plan for evaluating a staff development program that specifies the evaluation question(s), multiple data sources, data collection methodology, data analysis, interpretation, dissemination, and evaluation of the evaluation to assess the impact of the staff development program on student achievement.
Desired outcome: Evaluates school-based staff development programs using a variety of data.	▶ Arranges for the collection of student data (test scores, student surveys, and interviews) and classroom observation to determine changes in student learning and behaviors.
	▶ Arranges for teacher surveys, interviews, and observations to identify changes in classroom practices.
	▶ Assesses the extent to which school culture and organizational structures, policies, and processes have changed.
	▶ Identifies changes in teacher knowledge and skills that resulted from participation in staff development.
	▶ Collects information on participant satisfaction for each professional development session.
Desired outcome: Designs formative and summative evaluations of school-based professional development.	▶ Conducts both formative and summative evaluations of professional development.
	▶ Uses results to improve the program's quality as well as to identify the impact on teacher practices and student learning.

bulleted list of highlights. Oral reports might be as simple as a verbal summary in a meeting or as elaborate as a presentation with supporting slides, including charts.

Evaluate the evaluation. Few evaluations follow through with this final piece that examines the work of the evaluation itself. In a cycle of continuous improvement, an important element is to reflect and tweak essential components in order to determine ways to improve. By reviewing the evaluation process, team members will help ensure that the next evaluation will be even smoother.

Where to begin

▶ Determine team members' knowledge of and comfort with evaluations. Consult additional resources if needed.

▶ Assess whether the professional development is worth evaluating. Review Joellen Killion's eight steps in evaluation to gain clarity.

▶ Develop an evaluation plan. Determine whether to use formative evaluation, summative, or both. Decide what questions should be answered. Plan data collection and how results will be reported.

▶ Remember to schedule an evaluation of the evaluation.

Additional resources

American Evaluation Association. (2004, July). *Guiding principles for evaluators.* Available at www.eval.org/Publications/GuidingPrinciplesPrintable.asp.

Hall, G. & Hord, S. (2001). *Implementing change: Patterns, principles, and potholes.* Boston: Allyn & Bacon.

Joint Committee on Standards for Educational Evaluation. (2010, February). *Program evaluation standards.* Available at www.jcsee.org/program-evaluation-standards.

Joyce, B. & Showers, B. (2002). *Student achievement through staff development* (3rd ed.). Alexandria, VA: ASCD.

Killion, J. & Roy, P. (2009). *Becoming a learning school.* Oxford, OH: NSDC.

Kirkpatrick, D. (1994). *Evaluating training programs.* San Francisco: Berrett-Koehler Publishers.

Stiggins, R. (2001). *Student-involved classroom assessment* (3rd ed.). Upper Saddle River, NJ: Prentice Hall.

Tools index

TOOL	TITLE	USE
5.1	Measures that matter	**Tool 5.1** is an article that describes how a rural school district used assessments to gather data from multiple stakeholders to guide work in improving student achievement through focused instruction.
5.2	Weighing in	**Tool 5.2** describes how an urban school district used an online tool, the Standards Assessment Inventory (SAI), to measure whether teachers were experiencing high-quality professional learning. SAI results help identify which of NSDC's Standards for Staff Development to focus on to enhance the school's professional learning.
5.3	8 steps to improvement	**Tool 5.3** is an article about a suburban school district that embarked on learning and implementing an eight-step process for examining student data and adjusting instruction.
5.4	The evolution of a professional learning team	**Tool 5.4** provides a decision-making cycle to help learning teams stay focused during discussions and activities, offers a meeting overview checklist, describes four types of collaboration, and suggests an appropriate role for the learning team.
5.5	Facilitator: 10; refreshments: 8; evaluation: 0	**Tool 5.5** is an article that outlines the need for evaluation to be about more than satisfaction and to focus on what teachers are learning, what is being applied in the classroom, and how adult learning is improving student learning.
5.6	8 smooth steps	**Tool 5.6** is an article describing steps for planning and designing an in-depth evaluation of the impact of professional learning on improving teaching and student learning.

Tools index

TOOL	TITLE	USE
5.7	The real measure of a professional development program's effectiveness lies in what participants learn	**Tool 5.7** identifies practices that promote participants' learning and gives 10 suggestions for making a professional development program accountable.
5.8	Learning team survey	**Tool 5.8** allows learning teams to assess the benefits of participating in a team, team members' perceptions of their success in working in a team, changes in classroom practices based on team meetings, and more.
5.9	Clarify your vision with an Innovation Configuration map	**Tool 5.9** highlights the purpose of and how to develop an Innovation Configuration map. An IC map can be used as a tool to gather data from walk-throughs or to allow teachers to self-assess.
5.10	The age of our accountability	**Tool 5.10** is an article about the purpose of evaluation, three categories of evaluation, different levels of evaluation, and guidelines for a good evaluation.
5.11	Steps to your own evaluation	**Tool 5.11** helps guide planning the evaluation.
5.12	Evaluation framework	**Tool 5.12** is a sample evaluation plan, including evaluation questions to guide data collection methods and sources to use to monitor implementation and impact of the professional learning on teacher effectiveness and student achievement.
5.13	Level of understanding and degree of implementation survey	**Tool 5.13** is a sample survey for gathering baseline or pre- and post-implementation data to identify teachers' understanding and classroom implementation of the content of school-based professional learning.
5.14	Learning walk	**Tool 5.14** is a sample walk-through protocol for a leadership team to use to learn and reflect on members' understanding of the content focus of professional learning. The protocol also can be used to identify emerging patterns across the school and allow the team to use results to plan future professional learning.

"Individual commitment to a group effort — that is what makes a team work, a company work, society work, a civilization work."

— Vince Lombardi, American football coach

Chapter 6

CASE STUDY
of a school leadership team

This case study is a composite of the work of several real leadership teams from more than one district or area facing the issues that most teams do. Use this example to explore how the leadership team enacted change and planned a program of professional learning. As you read, consider what goes well and what might have been done better.

Consider the example on your own, or use it as a reflection tool with the leadership team by discussing the reflection questions posed at the close of this chapter.

GETTING STARTED

For more than a year, all the teachers at Beacon Middle School had been working in learning communities, the result of a districtwide initiative. Each week, students were dismissed early on Wednesday afternoon, and grade-level teams met every other week together. But at the end of the school year, principal Mary Bell did not see much difference in student achievement, especially in reading and with specific groups of students. As she looked over her notes from classroom observations and thought about the year, she concluded that she still saw widely varying quality of instruction.

In 6th grade, for example, she noted that the young, first-year teacher had taught an exceptional poetry unit, and students had produced some outstanding work. She smiled to herself as she remembered a particular poem that had really touched her, from a student who was a new immigrant and an English language learner. She had read his poem about his experience coming to the United States during the Veterans' Day assembly, and it had moved many adults to tears. Bell followed up her reflection with a little checking and found the other two 6th-grade teachers had not emphasized poetry much, although one of the 6th-grade standards for literacy was for all students to be able to read, view, and interpret texts from a variety of literary genres. While the teachers had noticed the student work posted in the hall, they had not really discussed it with the new teacher. "I think students already were taught poetry last year," one of the teachers told Bell when Bell asked. The other teacher said, "That just wasn't in my planning for the year. It's not emphasized on the 6th-grade standardized test."

Bell was also worried about the number of her school's students who were not performing well in high school freshman math courses. While she had no specific data, anecdotal evidence showed that students from the district's other feeder middle school fared better in high school math courses. The principal had a hallway conversation with the 8th-grade algebra teachers and found that, while they were working with the same materials, they had different approaches to testing. Both tested students at the end of each unit. One used multiple choice tests, and the other included word problems in his tests. The first teacher emphasized that multiple choice allowed her to get results back to the students quickly.

Bell felt some students still were falling through the cracks, and when she looked at the end-of-the-year student standardized test results, she was sure of it. The school did not make Adequate Yearly Progress in reading with special needs students, and the achievement gap with English language learners was significant. Many Hispanic students were performing poorly in reading. Bell was frustrated. Wasn't the districtwide emphasis on forming learning communities supposed to give teachers time to identify students' needs and find solutions? She'd tried to get into each learning team's meeting on a regular basis, but

other commitments often pulled her away. In those meetings she had attended, teachers often seemed burned out or had a lot of discussion about students without concluding anything about instructional practices.

Bell spent the first weeks after the school year ended connecting with colleagues within the district and researching online for ideas. She wanted to know their experiences with learning communities, what they were doing to address achievement gaps, and any new insights they'd had from their own professional learning. One colleague talked about school improvement planning, but Bell felt Beacon already had a school improvement plan in place that had taken a considerable amount of work to create. The thick binder was on the bookshelf in her office. Another colleague from within the district talked about having a leadership team of teachers who planned specific professional development with a collective focus for the whole faculty. Bell knew this principal well and had a great deal of respect for her. After more questions, Bell decided to form a school leadership team.

She carefully considered her faculty, their personal attributes, experience, and leadership qualities. She thought about who might get along well. She also considered diversity in gender, ages, experience, certification, and racial/ethnic background. After looking at numerous factors, she contacted five staff members from different grade levels and content areas, explained her plan, and asked if they would be willing to meet one full day and four half-days during a week in August before school started. She used building discretionary funds for stipends for the extra work.

Bell organized the first-day planning session in a little-used workroom in the school. She outlined her vision for the school leadership team and communicated her expectation that leadership team members would work together to support teachers in their professional learning communities and monitor teachers' progress in changing instructional practices based on intentional learning within their learning communities. As she handed out the agenda for the leadership team planning session, Bell invited team members to review the agenda items, ask questions, and suggest any additional items. Bell told the group that although they worked together in the same building, some worked at different grade levels and others might not know each other very well. She led a trust-building activity for teachers to get to know one another better. After the activity, she asked for a volunteer willing to facilitate a check-in/warm-up activity for the next meeting.

Bell told the group that to collaborate, they should develop norms. "Norms exist so that all team members may be explicit about the behaviors they expect from each other," Bell told the team. "Each team member should be willing to address a colleague's behavior that does not fit with the team's established norms, and focus on the behavior rather than the person to keep the team functioning smoothly. Norms will help you be more productive in your limited time together and will help you make your meetings efficient and effective."

The principal helped the group create a list of norms all members could agree to, and the group charted and signed the list: Start and end on time, come prepared, encourage everyone to participate, agree to disagree, ask questions, take a leadership role. Bell asked the team to be willing to adjust the list in future by adding or deleting behaviors. She reminded team members to post and refer to the norms during each of their meetings.

Next, Bell wanted teachers to form a common understanding around the team's work. She passed out copies of the article, "What is a professional learning community?" by Richard DuFour (2004), and asked them to read the definition and purpose of professional learning community. She used the Save the Last Word for Me protocol (see **Tool 2.1**) to engage the team

and prepare members to build consensus around a common understanding of a professional learning community and its purpose.

One team member volunteered to be the recorder and to capture ideas on a chart as the

> "Each team member should be willing to address a colleague's behavior that does not fit with the team's established norms, and focus on the behavior rather than the person to keep the team functioning smoothly."

teachers discussed what they learned and what they needed to focus on in terms of school and district expectations. From the article, they recorded that they would have to develop collaborative teams, focus on student learning, understand change, and overcome resistance. They wrote down three big ideas from the article: Ensure that students learn, create a culture of collaboration, and focus on results. They began discussing what they would need to know to lead school change and what would need to happen before school started. To Bell, they seemed a little overwhelmed.

To help the team visualize collaboration that focuses on student learning and results, the principal showed a DVD of a middle school team engaged in collaboration around a cycle of continuous improvement. Once again, the same team member volunteered to chart the team's discussion of what they learned from watching the DVD. Bell listened carefully. She wanted the teachers to infer a number of key points:

commitment to a collective responsibility for all students, use of a skilled facilitator, focus on student learning, analysis of teacher and student data to identify needs, the need for a plan for transfer of knowledge and skills to the classroom, and accountability for teacher implementation and student achievement results. The leadership team members wrote on their chart: Use data, review student work, follow up with what's happening in the classroom, results (with an exclamation point), and accountability (followed by a question mark).

KNOWLEDGE AND SKILLS

As the meeting progressed, team members talked more about their role with the existing professional learning communities. Their understanding of the leadership team's purpose began to crystallize. At this point, Bell asked the recorder to write a purpose statement, and the volunteer recorder wrote on a new piece of chart paper: The purpose of the leadership team is to lead the school change effort in implementing professional learning communities that impact teaching and learning.

After a lunch break together in the library, where Bell had arranged for food to be brought in, team members came back to the workroom. Bell asked them to spend five minutes journaling what they had learned in the morning and to note what questions they had. After the few moments of silence, the principal asked for their questions. Team members volunteered their thoughts, asking:

- Are the right people on the school leadership team? If not, who needs to be here? Do we need a special education teacher, the instructional coach, a teacher from each grade level, teachers from additional content areas?
- What is our time commitment as a member of this team? Will there be any stipend or compensation for the ongoing time?
- What knowledge and skills will we need to

be able to do this work? How will we learn what we need to know?
- Do we need a facilitator? Does anyone on the team have the expertise to facilitate? Do we need outside assistance?
- What resources are available to extend our own professional learning as teacher leaders?

A short discussion followed, and teachers began answering some of the questions themselves. They decided they wanted a particular teacher to join the team, one who was influential among the staff and whom they did not think they could do without. Bell had not included this teacher in the list, thinking to develop the leadership skills of others on her staff. The team members listed skills they thought they needed: data analysis and interpretation, writing SMART (specific, measurable, attainable, results-oriented, time-bound) goals, research-based instructional practices, assessments for learning, protocols for examining student work, facilitation and coaching skills. They listed needed resources such as time, funding, and materials.

ACTION PLANNING

The next item on Bell's agenda was action planning. After Bell opened the discussion with a definition of an action plan, team members quickly realized they should create a different type of action plan based on their new learning. Their action plan needed both a student achievement SMART goal and an adult professional learning goal based on identified student needs. They needed to chart their goals and write in results to help them focus on student and adult learning needs, identify professional learning that would help teachers gain knowledge and skills, include evidence of transfer to the collaborative teams/classrooms, and demonstrate impact on student achievement. See the chart they created in **Table 6.1**.

The teachers were satisfied with these first steps, and Bell said she thought they

Table 6.1: Action plan chart

SMART goal for student achievement:				
Adult professional learning goal:				
Student needs *(based on multiple sources of student data)*	**New knowledge and skills for teachers based on student needs**	**Plan for how teachers will learn new knowledge and skills**	**Evidence of implementation** *(teacher data on changed behaviors/ instructional practices)*	**Evidence of impact on student achievement** *(formative and summative student data)*

had accomplished a lot in one day, were clear on their purpose as a school leadership team in leading school change, had a common understanding of district and school expectations for implementing professional learning communities, and were beginning to understand the importance of short- and long-term planning focused on student results.

The principal led the group in reflecting on how well team members had adhered to the team norms, pointing to the chart as group members made comments that referenced a specific norm, and took ideas from the group to establish an agenda for the next meeting. As part of the agenda-setting process, Bell helped the team identify specific work to be done ahead

of the meeting and who would be responsible. Bell's assignment was to recruit the additional team member the group had identified for the school leadership team and to bring district and school student achievement data to the next day's meeting. The team members' assignments were to bring student data, including state assessment data, district benchmarking data, and classroom assessments, and to begin thinking of ideas for what the professional learning communities needed to know first and how best to engage their colleagues in intentional learning.

DATA RETREAT MEETING

The next day's meeting began with a warm-up activity led by the volunteer team member.

Then the team was ready to work. Team members understood now that they needed to focus on results and set measurable (SMART) goals for student achievement. They knew they would need to delve deeply into data to identify the highest priority student learning needs. Luckily for the school leadership team, Bell and most team members had attended a district data retreat in July. Some of the preliminary work of examining trends across the district and at the school was already done, work that had resulted in aligning district and school goals in reading with the district focus on a K-12 comprehensive literacy program.

Bell and the team spent two half-days comparing data and looking for trends. They prepared visual charts that helped them analyze the information. They divvied up tasks and worked in pairs to look at specific subscores in reading. They confirmed what Bell knew — that reading comprehension was an area in need of improvement — but they identified several specific skills in which students seemed weak and found through tracking the data that these were areas that historically had been weak as demonstrated through standardized assessments.

Although the school's improvement goal had been set in spring, the team decided the goal needed to be revisited and planned to do so the following day. Bell agreed to bring the binder from her office.

The next day, after another warm-up activity planned by a different team member, the group was feeling very comfortable and had the time team members needed before digging in to the work. They began by reviewing the school's existing school improvement goal. They decided the goal should be more specific for professional learning communities to focus on reading comprehension to increase student achievement for all students. The original school improvement goal stated: To increase the number of students scoring proficient in reading. The latest state testing showed 67% of students

scoring proficient. The school leadership team members worked together to write a new goal. They revised, edited, and finally agreed on a student achievement (SMART) goal: Within two years, 80% of all 6th- through 8th-grade students will score proficient or advanced in reading comprehension as measured by the district benchmark assessments and state standardized test in reading. The new goal also aligned with the district's emphasis on a K-12 comprehensive literacy program, team members noted. They felt pleased as they entered the SMART goal on the action plan chart.

At this point, most of the team members would have been ready to design professional development. However, looking at the planning chart and considering what they had learned in the past several meetings, they realized they should identify teacher needs before determining what professional learning was needed. The leadership team members began by identifying what teachers needed to know and be able to teach for greater student reading comprehension across different grade levels and content areas with a diverse student population.

One member of the team was a literacy specialist, had been part of the district literacy committee that planned how to implement the K-12 comprehensive literacy program, and had participated in professional development focused on reciprocal teaching. The literacy specialist told the group she had solid knowledge of a research-based instructional strategy that places teachers in small groups to work together to use prediction, questioning, clarifying, and summarization to understand text. The specialist went to her classroom and brought back the book *Improving Adolescent Literacy: Strategies at Work* by Douglas Fisher and Nancy Frey (2004) to help the school leadership team develop new knowledge and skills about literacy instruction across all content areas. Team members began by studying key points from the first chapter

Leadership team responsibilities

As teacher leaders, we will...

- Determine priorities aligned with student and adult learning goals and needs;

- Monitor progress in teacher implementation and student achievement;

- Problem solve; and

- Celebrate successes along the journey.

As learners, we will...

- Engage in ongoing professional learning during school leadership team meetings;

- Extend our knowledge and skills as needed within and outside the school related to reading comprehension, data analysis, facilitation, evaluation, and coaching.

As facilitators, we will...

- Use our skills with grade-level and subject professional learning teams;

- Model effective facilitation;

- Distribute leadership roles;

- Hold colleagues accountable through collection of and reflection on teacher and student data; and

- Act as liaisons between the grade-level teams and the school leadership team to ensure ongoing communication.

to help clarify where to begin the learning process with all teachers. As a result of their learning, the team wrote and agreed on an adult professional learning goal to help every teacher in the school narrow the focus on adult and student learning: To learn and apply one instructional strategy, reciprocal teaching, as a means of teaching comprehension to increase student achievement in reading for all groups.

With the two desired results filled in, the team found the rest of their action planning chart easy to complete. See what they wrote in **Table 6.2**.

The leadership team members began to feel they were becoming their own professional learning community. Now they needed to transfer their enthusiasm for learning and clarity in leading school change to the rest of the faculty.

A FINAL PLANNING DAY

The roles and responsibilities of being a school leadership team member were becoming clearer each time the group met as the week progressed. By the last day, Bell stepped back as group facilitator and suggested that another take on that role to distribute leadership further. The group decided through consensus to have one individual serve as facilitator for several months and then to rotate the role. The team decided to revisit the possibility of asking for

Table 6.2: Completed action plan chart

SMART goal (student achievement): Within two years, 80% of all 6th- through 8th-grade students will score proficient or advanced in reading comprehension as measured by the district benchmark assessments and state standardized test in reading.

Adult professional learning goal: To learn and apply one instructional strategy, reciprocal teaching, as a means of teaching comprehension to increase student achievement in reading for all groups.

Student needs *(based on multiple sources of student data)*	New knowledge and skills for teachers based on student needs	Plan for how teachers will learn new knowledge and skills	Evidence of implementation *(teacher data on changed behaviors/ instructional practices)*	Evidence of impact on student achievement *(formative and summative student data)*
Engage in understanding text in a variety of genres. Learn and apply four comprehension skills (prediction, questioning, clarifying, and summarization) to monitor own progress when reading text.	Understand the four comprehension skills (prediction, questioning, clarifying, and summarization) and how to engage students in using the four skills through reciprocal teaching. Model and monitor students' understanding of how to work in reciprocal teaching groups to help each other understand text. Use gradual release in helping students assume responsibility for their own learning.	Grade-level professional learning teams (biweekly during early release). Content-area teams (monthly). Faculty meetings. Coaching sessions. Learning walks. Book study.	Professional learning team logs. Lesson plans. Artifacts (charts, PowerPoint slides, graphic organizers) used in teaching four comprehension skills. Teacher observation checklist/notes during small group work. Student work samples. Principal/ leadership team walk-throughs.	Classroom assessments. District benchmarking assessments. State standardized test.

outside assistance each time the role was ready to rotate. Bell was pleased. Their decision allowed for teacher growth, provided some consistency for the group, and also recognized the possible need for additional support. She was even more pleased when the group suggested the social studies teacher take the role initially. Bell thought this teacher's quiet ways had meant her leadership qualities were less recognized by her peers.

As the teachers talked about their new responsibilities, they saw that their own process of gaining clarity on their role as part of the leadership team was a process their colleagues also would face. The leadership team members decided they needed to clearly articulate for themselves in writing as well as communicate to the whole faculty what their role would be in leading, learning, and facilitating change throughout the school year.

They spent another hour detailing their responsibilities. With a different, new volunteer recording notes, they wrote on the chart paper:

As teacher leaders, we will...

- Determine priorities aligned with student and adult learning goals and needs;
- Monitor progress in teacher implementation and student achievement;
- Problem solve; and
- Celebrate successes along the journey.

As learners, we will...

- Engage in ongoing professional learning during school leadership team meetings;
- Extend our knowledge and skills as needed within and outside the school related to reading comprehension, data analysis, facilitation, evaluation, and coaching.

As facilitators, we will...

- Use our skills with grade-level and subject professional learning teams;
- Model effective facilitation;
- Distribute leadership roles;

- Hold colleagues accountable through collection of and reflection on teacher and student data; and
- Act as liaisons between the grade-level teams and the school leadership team to ensure ongoing communication.

The team planned a school year kick-off with all the professional learning communities meeting simultaneously to send a positive message to the whole faculty that through working together, the staff could create a collective focus on success for all students.

FIRST PROFESSIONAL LEARNING TEAM MEETINGS

To begin the school year, the faculty gathered in the school library. Each professional learning team sat together at a table and listened as members of the leadership team briefly talked about their experience working in a group. One of the leadership team members showed the staff the chart the leadership team had written detailing the team's responsibilities.

Each school leadership team member then facilitated a group, modeling the learning that leadership team members had engaged in, including starting the meeting with a check-in to help group members get to know each other better. Each teacher shared something that had happened over the summer and stated an expectation for the new school year. The leadership team member reviewed the group's norms and helped members revise or set new norms, identifying behaviors that teachers wanted each other to honor to make their time together efficient and productive. The leadership team members then began the learning process with each professional learning group by revisiting student learning needs in reading comprehension and starting to focus on a common understanding around one instructional strategy, reciprocal teaching, with a focus on four comprehension skills (prediction, questioning, clarifying, and summarization).

Figure 6.1: Collaborative team log

COLLABORATIVE TEAM LOG

Grade level: Date: Time:

Team members present:

Reciprocal teaching focus: Circle comprehension skill focus for today.

      Prediction   Questioning   Clarifying   Summarization

Student achievement results: Look for patterns, identify students needing interventions.

Teacher learning focus: *Examples:* Examine student work, practice modeling a skill, read an article about reciprocal teaching/four comprehension skills, explore text to use for shared reading, design an assessment.

Class application:

Reflection of meeting (summary and review of behaviors):

Assignment for next meeting:

The first professional learning community team meeting ended with teachers reflecting on what worked and what didn't work for their teams and an assignment to read an article about reciprocal teaching and come to the next learning community meeting prepared to discuss what implementation would look like in their specific content area.

FOLLOW-UP LEADERSHIP TEAM MEETING

The school leadership team met before school on Friday at the end of the first week of school, without Bell, who was meeting with a parent, to reflect on members' experiences facilitating the professional learning community meetings and their successes and challenges. Knowing one of their responsibilities was to monitor progress, members designed a team log each could use and then collect to identify trends and help them monitor how teachers were implementing reciprocal teaching. See **Figure 6.1** for an example of the team log.

SECOND COLLABORATIVE TEAM MEETING

At the next early release day, professional learning teams again met. This time, the teams

Questions for reflection

- What key actions make the leadership team's work more likely to succeed?

- How might the leadership team better engage other faculty?

- What aspects of this team's work are exemplary?

- How does our leadership team function in ways similar to the example? How is what we do different from the case study?

- How much does context affect the way this leadership team functioned? How does our own context affect what we should be doing compared with the sample team?

- What are some next steps for the team in this example?

- How should the process that the team followed be tweaked for our own team?

- What outcomes should the example team expect? What outcomes do we expect for ourselves?

- Where can we make improvements in our own process based on what we have read and understood from this example?

- Highlight key ideas in the case study around how this leadership team functioned. Underline specific actions that struck you as you read. Volunteer your thoughts to the group about what you highlighted and underlined. Were these ideas and actions helpful to the leadership team? Were they likely to bring about success? In what ways could they be improved?

- Discuss the quote from Vince Lombardi at the opening of this chapter. What would this description look like if practiced on our team? In our school?

met in separate classrooms. The leadership team members again divided up and facilitated the individual professional learning communities.

In some of the meetings, teachers were frustrated and upset about participating in grade-level meetings that they felt were too structured and focused only on reciprocal teaching. Some teachers believed reading comprehension skills should be the responsibility only of language arts teachers and should not be the focus of their professional learning. They didn't understand a need for a collective focus on reading. School leadership team members in these groups made a mental note to raise teachers' concerns at the next school leadership team meeting. Most teachers brought the requested materials and engaged in productive work. Each team identified a recorder to complete the team log, and leadership team members were proud that they were beginning to model distributed leadership.

FOLLOW-UP MEETING

The school leadership team met the following Friday morning, an hour before student arrival. Team members brought their first professional learning community logs, and, as a team, members began to learn what information from the log was helpful in considering whole school improvement, what revisions might need to be made on the log format, and what feedback they felt the faculty needed to hear as a whole based on the data from the logs. In the short time the group had, their colleagues' resistance became a topic of discussion as they reflected on their experiences in the professional learning community meetings. They agreed to put the topic on the agenda for the next meeting.

Although each leadership team member and members of each grade-level professional learning community had different entry points to the improvement process, school leadership team members were confident that the school was heading in the right direction. They believed teachers were sharing leadership with the principal to implement and monitor school-based professional learning that was relevant and embedded in teachers' daily work.

Tools index

TOOL	TITLE	USE
6.1	Collaborative team log	**Tool 6.1** is a sample collaborative team log that the school leadership team and collaborative learning teams can use to record and monitor adult and student learning focus and results.
6.2	Sample school leadership team responsibilities	**Tool 6.2** is a sample list of responsibilities for teacher leaders, learners, and facilitators.

Appendix A

PROTOCOLS
for reading articles

Protocols are processes that help team members engage in dialogue to understand text in depth, to explore current teaching practices, to examine student work or results from assessments, or to surface problems or issues related to implementation of professional learning. Protocols vary in purpose and amount of time needed; however, they provide the means for focused, more in-depth professional discussion and different points of view.

Protocols provide structure, which includes different roles (e.g. facilitator, presenter, time keeper), specific timed steps to maintain focus on the topic and allow for more depth in understanding as a result of the discussion, and norms so participants know when to speak and when to listen (Allen & Blythe, 2004; Easton, 2009).

The protocols in the appendix align with the resources in this book.

For additional information, some useful resources include:

- **Allen, D. & Blythe, T. (2004).** *The facilitator's book of questions: Tools for looking together at student and teacher work.* New York: Teachers College Press.

- **Easton, L. (2009, February/March).** Protocols: A facilitator's best friend. *Tools for Schools, 12(*3), 1-3.

- **Easton, L. (2009).** *Protocols for professional learning.* Alexandria, VA: ASCD.

- **Killion, J. & Roy, P. (2009).** *Becoming a learning school.* Oxford, OH: NSDC.

- **National School Reform Faculty.** www.nsrfharmony.org.

Three levels of text

Purpose: To construct meaning collaboratively, and to clarify and expand thinking about a text, from written document to videotape to podcast, using increasingly specific descriptions.

Time: As little as 20 minutes depending on the size of the group or extended for as long as there is time. (It should be extended if the text is long and complex or if there are more than 10 people in a group.)

Materials: Text, such as "Professional Learning in the Learning Profession: A Status Report on Teacher Development in the U.S. and Abroad," available in the Chapter 2 tools on the CD accompanying this book.

PREPARATION

The ideal group is six to 10 people. Divide larger groups and select a facilitator for each table group, along with a room facilitator to keep time and move the group along. Designate a recorder to chart ideas. Have participants read, view, or listen to the text, taking notes.

DIRECTIONS

1. **Sentences** *(about 10 minutes)*
    Each member of the group shares a sentence from the text or from his/her notes about something that struck that person as particularly significant. Others listen and perhaps take notes. There is no discussion.

2. **Phrases** *(about 10 minutes)*
    Each person shares a phrase from the text or from notes written about the text on something that struck that person as significant. Others listen and perhaps take notes. There is no discussion.

3. **Words** *(about 10 minutes)*
    Each person shares a word from the text or from notes written about the text on something that struck that person as significant. Others listen and perhaps take notes. There is no discussion.

4. **Discussion** *(about 10 minutes)*
    Group members discuss what they heard and learned about the text being studied. The group discusses which words emerged and new insights about the document.

5. **Debriefing** *(about 5 minutes)*
    The group debriefs the process.

Descriptive review process: *Learning from student work*

The Descriptive Review Process asks teachers to look together at pieces of student work, to discuss what they see in the work, and to bring multiple perspectives to an analysis of the work in order to improve the quality of the work designed for and produced by students.

STEP 1. GETTING STARTED

The group chooses a facilitator to keep the group focused. The presenting teacher distributes copies of the selected student work or displays the work. At this point, the teacher says nothing about the work, its context, or the student. Participants read or observe the work in silence, making notes if they choose.

STEP 2. DESCRIBING THE WORK

The facilitator asks, "What do you see?" Participants respond without making judgments about the work.

STEP 3. RAISING QUESTIONS

The facilitator asks, "What questions does this work raise for you?" The presenting teacher makes notes but does not yet respond.

STEP 4. SPECULATING ABOUT THE WORK

The facilitator asks, "What do you think the student is working on?" Participants offer ideas.

STEP 5. PRESENTING TEACHER RESPONDS

At the facilitator's invitation, the presenting teacher tells about the work, responds to questions, and comments on unexpected things that he or she heard in the group's responses and questions.

STEP 6. DISCUSSING IMPLICATIONS FOR DESIGNING STUDENT WORK AND STUDENT LEARNING

The group and the presenting teacher discuss ways to improve the design of the work.

Adapted from *The Collaborative Assessment Conference*, by Steve Seidel and Harvard University's Project Zero, 1988.

Say something protocol

Purpose: This protocol engages readers with text as they read. This tool is useful when team members will be reading at a meeting and using text to inform.

Time: Varies according to selected reading material.

Materials: Copy of the text for each participant.

DIRECTIONS

1. Partners each read silently up to a designated point.

2. Once the stopping point is reached, each partner speaks in order to build connections, offer examples, ask questions, etc. Suggestions for partners' talking points are:
   - Something I agree with.
   - Something that puzzles me.
   - Something I am reminded of when I read . . .
   - A new idea.
   - Something I disagree with.
   - Something I want the author to explain more.
   - Something I want to talk more about with others.

3. Partners continue reading sections and pausing to speak until they complete the selection.

4. The whole group discusses the text.

Source: Adapted from the National School Reform Network, www.nsfrharmony.org.

Norms for text-based protocols

Purpose: To develop norms around how to have group conversation using articles and other resources that support team development.

Time: 15 to 30 minutes, depending on group size.

Materials: Copy of the sample norms.

DIRECTIONS

1. Use the sample norms below as a start to develop the team's own list.

2. Post the norms, and practice with them while using a protocol.

3. Revisit the list periodically to check whether adjustments are needed to the list or to the group's practice.

SAMPLE NORMS

- Be an active listener.
- Agree to be an active participant — one of the responsibilities of group membership.
- Be comfortable with silence and pauses to allow for reflection.
- Allow each individual time to speak.
- Build on what others say. Avoid starting a sentence with "But…" or "I disagree…"
- One person speaks at a time.
- Speak directly to one another, not through another.
- Focus on the person speaking without interrupting or distracting from his/her point either verbally or with body language.
- Be aware of your assumptions and state them.
- Keep comments focused on the reading and refer to the text, not to an individual.
- Limit your own comment time to allow for broad discussion and sharing of ideas.
- Indicate the page and paragraph you are quoting from before you read it.

Source: Adapted from National School Reform Faculty, www.nsrfharmony.org, as developed by Gene Thompson-Grove.

Framing question

Purpose: To push team members' thinking in new directions around the substance of a text.

Time: 30 minutes to 60 minutes, depending on group size and reading.

Materials: Copy of the article for each participant.

DIRECTIONS

1. Ahead of time, designate one person to facilitate the session in which the group will discuss the article. This person will be responsible for creating a framing question that requires team members to carefully read the text for an answer. Make the question as literal and deep as the purpose of the selected reading. As the team develops, questions could include responding to quotes, identifying assumptions and patterns, or reflecting on values. The facilitator should be prepared with a few follow-up questions to push the group's thinking and keep the conversation going if it stalls.

2. Post the guiding question in plain sight of everyone in the group.

3. Before the group begins, review the purpose of reading the particular selection. Review the group's norms.

4. Allow the group about five minutes per page to read the selection.

5. Facilitate the conversation by first stating the question, then allowing and guiding responses. Refer to group norms to encourage each member to speak and no individual to dominate.

Source: Adapted from National School Reform Faculty, www.nsrfharmony.org.

Degrees of feedback

Purpose: To determine the group's reaction to a selection and how the reading may apply to a particular context.

Time: 30 minutes to 60 minutes, depending on group size and reading.

Materials: Copy of the article for each participant.

DIRECTIONS

1. Have the group read the selected text, allowing about five minutes for each page.

2. In round-robin fashion, with each round focused on a different type of feedback, ask each member to comment as follows:
   - **Warm:** What were the positive points in what you read? What did you respond to as a desirable idea?
   - **Cool:** What in the reading raised doubts for you? What questions arose for you from this selection?
   - **Hard:** What challenges do you see related to the purpose of this selection? How do you see these challenges in our own context?

What do you see?

Purpose: To engage group members in a closer reading of a text.

Time: 30 minutes to 60 minutes, depending on group size and reading.

Materials: Copy of the article for each participant.

DIRECTIONS

1. Ahead of time, designate one person to open the session in which the group will discuss the article. This person reads the article in advance.

2. The designated opener introduces the article briefly and allows the group five minutes per page to read the selection. The opener may use this time to outline his or her reactions: feasible, challenging, unrealistic.

3. The opener states his or her questions or opinions about the article or highlights provocative ideas.

4. The opener then asks each group member to summarize the article as literally as possible.

5. The opener then asks specific questions, such as:
   - What are the underlying values of what's outlined in the article?
   - What assumptions are present?
   - What is our purpose in reading this selection?
   - What skills/knowledge are in evidence? Which are present in our school? Which are needed?
   - What do we need to know or understand to be able to … ?
   - How is our work similar or different from what is presented?
   - What aspects of this work are attractive to us?
   - What obstacles might we face in pursuing these actions? What would we do to work around these?

6. Group members take turns reacting and adding to the ideas raised.

7. The opener or a designated recorder tracks main ideas and summarizes them for the group.

8. The group works jointly to develop any suggestions or recommendations for action based on the reading.

Silence/talk

Purpose: To exchange ideas, understand the wisdom of the collective group, solve problems, plan, or allow for more complete participation without conflict.

Time: Up to 60 minutes, depending on group size and reading.

Materials: Copy of the article for each participant, markers, chart paper, tape.

DIRECTIONS

1. Post paper on the walls ahead of the meeting.

2. Have one person open the session by announcing that the activity will be completed in silence. One person can comment on another's ideas by drawing.

3. Post a question in a circle on the board. The question may be prepared in advance by a facilitator, a volunteer, or an external leader. The question should relate to the purpose of the reading. The level of depth of the question will determine the usefulness of the activity. For example, "What do you think the connection is between professional learning communities and student achievement?" or "How might we improve learning at our school using …." may elicit more conversation than, "What did the school in the example do well?"

4. Each participant takes a marker and begins to brainstorm on the paper. Participants may create headings, such as "What I'd like to know more about…" or "Statements from the text I agree with."

5. Individuals add to one another's comments or drawings, circle ideas they are interested in, note questions about any comments, and draw connectors between ideas or themes.

6. After allowing enough time for all to finish thoughtfully, including what may be pauses or lulls, the group then discusses the result.

The four A's

Purpose: To engage group members in a closer reading of a text.

Time: 30 minutes to 60 minutes, depending on group size and reading.

Materials: Copy of the article for each participant.

DIRECTIONS

1. Post four questions in sight of all participants:
   - What assumptions underlie the text?
   - What do you agree with in the text?
   - What part of the text do you want to argue with?
   - What in the text do you aspire to?

2. Ask each participant to read the text silently and highlight striking sections, make notes in the margin, or use sticky notes to answer the four questions.

3. Allow each participant to respond to the questions, one question at a time, referencing the reading.

4. Allow time for open discussion.

5. Debrief.

Source: National School Reform Faculty, www.nsrfharmony.org.

Block party

Purpose: To engage group members in a closer reading of a text. This works well with larger groups.

Time: 30 minutes to 60 minutes, depending on group size and reading.

Materials: Index cards, copy of the article for each participant.

DIRECTIONS

1. Select a facilitator ahead of the session. The facilitator prepares by writing quotes on index cards. Some quotes may be repeated or each may be different, but the number should be divisible by the number of participants in the group.

2. Have participants randomly select an index card and reflect on the quote for several minutes.

3. Ask group members to pair off to read one another the quote and share reactions.

4. Form groups of three or four to share quotes and insights, as well as implications for the team's work.

5. Share responses as a whole group, including ideas and questions raised.

6. Provide the article to participants to see the source of the quotes.

7. Debrief.

Alternatives include having participants exchange index cards after each round and including a step asking participants to speculate on the origin and purpose of the quotes.

Source: National School Reform Faculty, www.nsrfharmony.org.

The final word

Purpose: To give each participant an opportunity to be heard on his or her ideas about a text and to enhance the group's understanding by hearing from all members.

Time: About eight minutes for each participant in the group.

Materials: Copy of the article for each participant.

DIRECTIONS

1. Designate a facilitator and a timekeeper, who also participates.

2. Ask group members to read the text ahead of time and to underline or highlight one significant idea.

3. Form a circle. Have one person read his or her highlighted item and describe why he or she selected this quote (i.e. what she wonders about, what he disagrees with, what issues are raised). The timekeeper allows three minutes.

4. Each participant takes one minute or less to respond to the quote and reader's reaction. The purpose of the response is to:
   - Expand on the presenter's thinking about the quote and issues raised.
   - Provide a different perspective on the quote.
   - Clarify the presenter's thinking.
   - Ask clarifying questions about the quote.
   - Question the presenter's assumptions about the quote.

5. Allow the person who presented the quote to have the final word. How has his or her thinking changed? What is his or her reaction to what others have said?

6. Have the next person present a quote and follow the same format until each person has had a turn.

Source: National School Reform Faculty, www.nsrfharmony.org.

Jigsaw readings

Purpose: The jigsaw enables a group to read a lengthy article quickly. However, the facilitator must prepare ahead of time by dividing the article into appropriate sections. Adapt the process depending on the number of participants, the size of the reading, or next steps.

Materials: Sufficient copies of the article for each participant.

Time: Varies, depending on the reading material. Maximum: 60 minutes.

DIRECTIONS

1. Divide the article or book chapter into smaller pieces.

2. Ensure that the number of short reading selections matches the number of small reading groups. *(Depending on the size of your group, you may want to have one individual read each section.)*

3. Assign a short reading to each small group and have the groups read their assigned selections. (Another option: Count off by the number of passages you have selected and assign the readings in that fashion.)

4. Gather together the individuals who read the same passages, and allow them time to discuss what they read and to share their ideas and insights. Depending on how you want to synthesize the material, ask participants to identify three to five key ideas to report to the larger group.

5. Bring the larger group together and have each team report on what members learned, allowing time for questions.

This activity can be adapted to be used during a pre-meeting or "homework" assignment for a group.

Appendix B

INNOVATION
Configuration maps

One of the tools from the Concerns-Based Adoption Model (CBAM) that can be used to monitor change is the Innovation Configuration (IC) map. An IC map describes the behavior one would observe in variations of a practice. The variations are identified as levels on the IC map, with the ideal level (Level 1) always on the left. The levels provide users with a progression of steps needed to achieve the ideal (Level 1) for each area or desired outcome.

An individual or team can use the IC map as a planning or assessment tool. For planning, the leadership team can use a comparison of current practice with the IC maps to develop specific actions for progressing on the continuum toward Level 1, desired outcome. As an assessment tool, the leadership team can identify a teacher or group's current state

Additional information on using the maps is available in:

- **Hord, S., Hirsh, S., & Roy, P. (2003).** *Moving NSDC's staff development standards into practice: Innovation configurations, Volume I.* Oxford, OH: NSDC.

- **Killion, J. & Roy, P. (2009).** *Becoming a learning school.* Oxford, OH: NSDC.

- **Killion, J. & Harrison, C. (2006).** *Taking the lead: New roles for teachers and school-based coaches.* Oxford, OH: NSDC.

- **National Staff Development Council. (2001).** *NSDC's standards for staff development.* Oxford, OH: Author.

of understanding and implementation of the identified desired outcomes for the specific IC map.

IC maps have been developed to monitor implementation of NSDC's definition of high-quality professional learning and NSDC's Standards for Staff Development. This appendix includes select IC maps for school-based professional development leaders to use as planning and assessment tools. Maps are included for a Learning School as well as for the Learning Communities, Leadership, Resources, Evaluation, Design, Collaboration, and Quality Teaching standards.

Learning School
Innovation Configuration map

The Learning School Innovation Configuration map is a planning and assessment tool for use by school leadership teams and collaborative professional learning teams to ensure full implementation of NSDC's definition of professional development and the system structures needed to support collaborative professional learning. Learning schools work to achieve Level 1 in each component area over time.

An Innovation Configuration (IC) map describes in behavioral terms what key stakeholders do in a learning school. It also describes variations of the ideal or best practices in a learning school along a continuum that describes the progression schools make over time along the road to become a learning school. As a planning tool, the IC map guides a school's leadership team and teams of teachers in the identification of specific actions to progress toward the desired outcome. As an assessment tool, the IC map serves as a guide to determine the current state of the school's implementation of the definition. The planning and assessment functions of the IC map work hand-in-hand to guide school leadership teams and collaborative professional learning teams to establish the context and processes of effective learning schools.

COMPREHENSIVE, SUSTAINED, INTENSIVE PROFESSIONAL LEARNING

Outcome 1: In a learning school, the school leadership team, teacher leaders (coaches), teams of teachers, and individual teachers engage in effective professional learning.

EFFECTIVENESS

1.1: The school leadership team, teacher leaders (coaches), teams of teachers, and individual teachers engage in comprehensive, sustained, and intensive professional learning to improve teachers' and principals' effectiveness in raising student achievement.

Level 1	Level 2	Level 3	Level 4	Level 5	Level 6
Engage in intentional, comprehensive, sustained, and intensive professional learning focused on raising student achievement by improving teaching quality and leadership.	Engage in intentional, comprehensive, sustained, and intensive professional learning focused on raising student achievement by improving teaching quality.	Engage in intentional, comprehensive, sustained, and intensive professional learning focused on multiple topics.	Engage in short-term, intentional, professional learning focused on raising student achievement by improving teaching quality and leadership.	Engage in short-term, intentional, professional learning focused on raising student achievement by improving teaching quality.	Engage in occasional, intentional, professional learning focused on a variety of topics.

COLLECTIVE RESPONSIBILITY

1.2: The school leadership team, teacher leaders (coaches), teams of teachers, and individual teachers share collective responsibility for student learning.

Level 1	Level 2	Level 3	Level 4	Level 5	Level 6
Work and learn together sharing collective responsibility so that each individual and team contributes to the success of ALL students within the school.	Work and learn together sharing collective responsibility so that each team contributes to the success of its students.	Work and learn together so that each individual team member can improve the success of his or her students.	Acknowledge that they have limited responsibility for student learning.	Hold nonschool factors responsible for student performance.	Disregard factors that influence student academic success.

TEAM CONFIGURATION

1.3: The school leadership team, teacher leaders (coaches), teams of teachers, and individual teachers meet in a variety of team configurations over time addressing specific goals for teacher and student learning.

Level 1	Level 2	Level 3	Level 4	Level 5	Level 6
Meet in a variety of team configurations over time, addressing specific goals for teacher and student learning, including vertical and whole-school problem or topic-focused school improvement teams and grade-level, department, or course teams with members who share common curriculum and/or students.	Meet in a variety of team configurations over time, addressing specific goals for teacher and student learning, including grade-level, department, or course teams with members who share common curriculum or students, or project teams for school improvement.	Meet in a variety of team configurations over time, addressing specific goals for teacher and student learning, including grade-level, department, or course teams.	Meet over time in a single team, addressing specific goals for teacher and student learning, school improvement, and student results.	Work independently addressing specific goals for teacher and student learning.	Work independently without focus on specific goals for teacher and student learning.

FREQUENCY

1.4: The school leadership team, teacher leaders (coaches), teams of teachers, and individual teachers make time for professional learning several times per week.

Level 1	Level 2	Level 3	Level 4	Level 5	Level 6
Meet several times per week within the school day for teacher collaborative team meetings and periodic whole-school collaboration.	Meet each week within the school day for teacher collaborative team meetings and periodic whole-school collaboration.	Meet biweekly within the school day for teacher collaborative team meetings and periodic whole-school collaboration.	Meet each month within the school day for teacher collaborative team meetings and periodic whole-school collaboration.	Meet several days per school year within the school day for teacher collaborative team meetings and whole-school collaboration.	Meet outside the school day for teacher collaborative meetings and whole-school collaboration.

CONTINUOUS CYCLE OF IMPROVEMENT

Outcome 2: Learning teams use a cycle of continuous improvement to refine teaching quality and improve student learning.

DATA ANALYSIS

2.1: Learning teams engage in ongoing data analysis of teacher and student performance to determine school, educator, and student learning goals.

Level 1	Level 2	Level 3	Level 4	Level 5	Level 6
Analyze multiple types of data (achievement, process, demographic, and perception) at the school, team, and classroom levels throughout the school year to identify student strengths and weaknesses to set annual goals for student growth and teacher learning; analyze multiple types of data at the school, team, and classroom levels several times throughout the school year to measure progress toward annual goals for student and teacher learning, to set benchmark goals for teacher and student learning, and to make ongoing adjustments in both goals and strategies for attaining the goals.	Analyze student achievement and demographic data at the school, team, and classroom levels throughout the school year to identify student strengths and weaknesses to set annual goals for student growth and teacher learning; analyze student achievement and demographic data at the school, team, and classroom levels several times throughout the school year to measure progress toward annual goals for student and teacher learning, to set benchmark goals for teacher and student learning, and to make ongoing adjustments in both goals and strategies for attaining the goals.	Analyze student achievement data at the school, team, and classroom levels throughout the school year to identify student strengths and weaknesses to set annual goals for student growth and teacher learning; analyze student achievement data at the school, team, and classroom levels several times throughout the school year to measure progress toward annual goals for student and teacher learning, to set benchmark goals for teacher and student learning, and to make ongoing adjustments in both goals and strategies for attaining the goals.	Analyze student achievement data at the school level throughout the school year to identify student strengths and weaknesses to set annual goals for student growth and teacher learning; analyze student achievement data at the school, team, and classroom levels several times throughout the school year to measure progress toward annual goals for student and teacher learning, and to set benchmark goals for teacher and student learning.	Analyze student achievement data at the school level throughout the school year to identify student strengths and weaknesses to set annual goals for student growth and teacher learning; analyze student achievement data at the school, team, and classroom levels several times throughout the school year to measure progress toward annual goals for student and teacher learning.	Analyze student achievement data at the school level throughout the school year to identify student strengths and weaknesses to set annual goals for student growth.

STUDENT LEARNING GOALS

2.2: Learning teams set goals for student learning.

Level 1	Level 2	Level 3	Level 4	Level 5	Level 6
Write annual and benchmark SMART (specific, measurable, attainable, results-oriented, time-bound) goals for student achievement based on school, team, and classroom data to guide their planning and improvement efforts and revise those goals throughout the school year.	Write annual SMART (specific, measurable, attainable, results-oriented, time-bound) goals for student achievement based on school, team, and classroom data to guide their planning and improvement efforts and revise those goals throughout the school year.	Write annual SMART (specific, measurable, attainable, results-oriented, time-bound) goals for student achievement based on school, team, and classroom data to guide their planning and improvement efforts.	Receive annual SMART (specific, measurable, attainable, results-oriented, time-bound) goals for student achievement based on schoolwide data to guide their planning and improvement efforts.	Receive annual SMART (specific, measurable, attainable, results-oriented, time-bound) goals for student achievement based on districtwide data to guide their planning and improvement efforts.	Receive annual goals for student achievement based on districtwide data to guide their planning and improvement efforts.

EDUCATOR LEARNING GOALS

2.3: Learning teams write goals for educator learning aligned with student learning goals to guide professional learning.

Level 1	Level 2	Level 3	Level 4	Level 5	Level 6
Write annual and benchmark professional learning goals for the school and teams aligned with student learning goals and revise those goals throughout the school year.	Write annual and benchmark professional learning goals for the school and teams aligned with student learning goals.	Write annual professional learning goals for the school aligned with student learning goals.	Use district professional learning goals to guide adult learning within the school and team.	Use district professional learning goals to guide adult learning within the school.	Use topics rather than goals to guide professional learning within the school.

MULTIPLE DESIGNS

2.4: Learning teams select and implement multiple designs for professional learning aligned with NSDC's Standards for Staff Development to develop knowledge, attitudes, skills, aspirations, and behaviors necessary to support advanced levels of student learning.

Level 1	Level 2	Level 3	Level 4	Level 5	Level 6
Select, with broad-based input from teacher leaders and teachers, and implement multiple selected designs for team and whole-school professional learning that align with educator and student learning goals and support and encourage collaborative inquiry, problem solving, and learning among educators.	Select, with broad-based input from teacher leaders and teachers, and implement two selected designs for team and whole-school professional learning that align with educator and student learning goals and support and encourage collaborative inquiry, problem solving, and learning among educators.	Select, with broad-based input from teacher leaders and teachers, and implement a single design for team and whole-school professional learning that align with educator and student learning goals and support and encourage collaborative inquiry, problem solving, and learning among educators.	Implement multiple selected designs for team and whole-school professional learning aligned with student learning goals with limited input from teacher leaders and teachers.	Implement a single design for team and whole-school professional learning aligned with student learning goals with limited input from teacher leaders and teachers.	Implement designs for team- and whole-school professional learning selected by someone outside the school without input from teacher leaders and teachers.

INTERVENTIONS FOR STUDENT LEARNING

2.5: Learning teams select or develop research-based, coherent, classroom-centered interventions for student learning.

Level 1	Level 2	Level 3	Level 4	Level 5	Level 6
Select and/or develop research-based, coherent, classroom-centered interventions for student learning that align with team and student learning goals, focus on the school's instructional framework for teaching quality, and emphasize changes in teacher practice to promote student learning.	Select and/or develop research-based, coherent, classroom-centered interventions for student learning that align with team and student learning goals and focus on the school's instructional framework for teaching quality.	Select and/or develop research-based, coherent, classroom-centered interventions for student learning that align with team and student learning goals.	Select and/or develop classroom-centered interventions for student learning that align with team and student learning goals.	Select and/or develop school-centered interventions for student learning that align with team and student learning goals.	Select and/or develop nonclassroom- and nonschool-centered interventions for student learning.

JOB-EMBEDDED SUPPORT

2.6: The school leadership team, teacher leaders (coaches), and team members provide ongoing support at the classroom level to implement educator learning to increase student achievement.

Level 1	Level 2	Level 3	Level 4	Level 5	Level 6
Provide continuous job-embedded coaching and other forms of classroom-based support (e.g. peer observation, instructional, walk-throughs, demonstration lessons, etc.) to transfer educator learning to classroom and schoolwide practice to increase student achievement.	Provide periodic job-embedded coaching and other forms of classroom-based support (e.g. peer observation, instructional, walk-throughs, demonstration lessons, etc.) to transfer educator learning to classroom and schoolwide practice to increase student achievement.	Provide occasional job-embedded coaching and other forms of classroom-based support (e.g. peer observation, instructional, walk-throughs, demonstration lessons, etc.) to transfer educator learning to classroom and schoolwide practice to increase student achievement.	Provide one opportunity for job-embedded coaching and other forms of classroom-based support (e.g. peer observation, instructional, walk-throughs, demonstration lessons, etc.) to transfer educator learning to classroom and schoolwide practice to increase student achievement.	Provide no job-embedded coaching or other forms of classroom-based support (e.g. peer observation, instructional, walk-throughs, demonstration lessons, etc.) to transfer educator learning to classroom and schoolwide practice to increase student achievement.	

ONGOING EVALUATION

2.7: Learning teams evaluate the effectiveness of professional learning.

Level 1	Level 2	Level 3	Level 4	Level 5	Level 6
Assess regularly (multiple times per year) the effectiveness of professional learning in achieving identified educator and student learning goals, improving teaching, and assisting all students in meeting academic standards.	Assess semiannually the effectiveness of professional learning in achieving identified educator and student learning goals, improving teaching, and assisting all students in meeting academic standards.	Assess annually the effectiveness of professional learning in achieving identified educator and student learning goals, improving teaching, and assisting all students in meeting academic standards.	Assess over multiple years the effectiveness of professional learning in achieving identified educator and student learning goals, improving teaching, and assisting all students in meeting academic standards.	Conduct no assessment of the effectiveness of professional learning in achieving identified educator and student learning goals, improving teaching, and assisting all students in meeting academic standards.	

EXPANDED OPPORTUNITIES FOR PROFESSIONAL LEARNING

Outcome 3: In a learning school, the school leadership team, teacher leaders (coaches), and teacher teams access external assistance to provide teams with expanded opportunities for professional learning, additional resources, and expert guidance to support team learning and goal attainment.

EXTERNAL ASSISTANCE

3.1: Learning teams, school leadership teams, and teacher leaders (coaches) access external assistance to extend educator and student learning goals.

Level 1	Level 2	Level 3	Level 4	Level 5	Level 6
Access external assistance providers within and outside the school system to support the implementation of collaborative professional learning and help the team reach its professional learning goals and student learning goals by expanding opportunities within the school for professional learning, sharing resources, offering guidance, and assessing effectiveness and impact.	Access external assistance providers within and outside the school system to support the implementation of collaborative professional learning and help the team reach its professional learning goals and student learning goals by expanding opportunities outside the school for professional learning, sharing resources, offering guidance, and assessing effectiveness and impact.	Access external assistance providers within and outside the school system to support the implementation of collaborative professional learning and help the team reach its professional learning goals and student learning goals by expanding opportunities outside the school for professional learning.	Access external assistance providers within and outside the school system to support the implementation of collaborative professional learning and help the team reach its student learning goals.	Access external assistance providers within and outside the school system to support the implementation of collaborative professional learning and assist the team in reaching its professional learning goals.	Access no external assistance to support the implementation of collaborative professional learning, team learning goals, individual learning goals, or student learning goals.

CHANGE, LEAD, SUCCEED

LEARNING OUTSIDE THE SCHOOL

3.2: The school leadership team, teacher leaders (coaches), teams of teachers, and individual teachers participate in learning outside the school.

Level 1	Level 2	Level 3	Level 4	Level 5	Level 6
Participate in professional learning offered by the central office or organizations outside the school district when there is clear evidence that the learning aligns with a team or school learning goal and there is a commitment to apply the learning schoolwide, in teams, or in classrooms as appropriate, and to assess the impact of such actions.	Participate in professional learning offered by the central office or organizations outside the school district when there is clear evidence that the learning aligns with a team or school learning goal and there is a commitment to apply the learning schoolwide, in teams, or classroom as appropriate.	Participate in professional learning offered by the central office or organizations outside the school district when there is clear evidence that the learning aligns with a team or school learning goal.	May participate in learning events offered by the central office and/or organizations outside the school district.	May participate in learning events offered by the central office.	Participate in no learning events outside the school.

EVALUATION OF COLLABORATIVE PROFESSIONAL LEARNING

Outcome 4: In learning schools, the school leadership team, teacher leaders (coaches), and teacher teams evaluate the collaborative professional learning to make improvements.

ONGOING EVALUATION

4.1: The school leadership team, teacher leaders (coaches), teams of teachers, and individual teachers evaluate collaborative professional learning on an ongoing basis.

Level 1	Level 2	Level 3	Level 4	Level 5	Level 6
Engage in ongoing evaluation using multiple sources of data to assess team results, operations, and individual members' contribution to teams and to adjust their efforts.	Engage in ongoing evaluation using a single source of data to assess team results, operations and individual members' contribution to teams and to adjust their efforts.	Engage in ongoing evaluation using multiple sources of data to assess team results and operations and to adjust their efforts.	Engage in ongoing evaluation using multiple sources of data to assess team results and operations.	Engage in intermittent evaluation to assess team results, operations, and individual members' contribution to teams.	Engage in intermittent evaluation to assess team results and operations.

SCHOOL SUPPORT FOR COLLABORATIVE PROFESSIONAL LEARNING

Outcome 5: In learning schools, principals, teacher leaders (coaches), and teachers support staff collaboration.

PRINCIPAL SUPPORT

5.1: Principals set expectations for, support, monitor, and evaluate collaborative professional learning.

Level 1	Level 2	Level 3	Level 4	Level 5	Level 6
Set expectations for all staff to engage in collaborative professional learning; provide support for teams; ensure that teams have professional learning on effective team functioning; monitor team plans, goals, and progress; meet periodically with teams to assess their operation; meet regularly with team leaders to discuss teams' work and progress; review team logs; and hold regular cross-team meetings to share what teams are learning for the benefit of the whole faculty.	Set expectations for all staff to engage in collaborative professional learning; ensure that teams have professional learning on effective team functioning; monitor team plans, goals, and progress; monitor team plans, goals, and progress by participating in team meetings and meeting with team leaders to discuss team processes and outcomes.	Set expectations for all staff to engage in collaborative professional learning; provide support for teams; ensure that teams have professional learning on effective team functioning; monitor team plans, goals, and progress by meeting periodically with teams to assess their operation and by reviewing team logs.	Set expectations for all staff to engage in collaborative professional learning; ensure that teams have professional learning on effective team functioning; monitor team plans, goals, and progress by reviewing team logs.	Set expectations for all staff to engage in collaborative professional learning; monitor team plans, goals, and progress by reviewing team logs.	Set expectations for all staff to engage in collaborative professional learning.

TEACHER LEADER SUPPORT

5.2: In learning schools, teacher leaders (coaches) support collaborative professional learning.

Level 1	Level 2	Level 3	Level 4	Level 5	Level 6
Facilitate team data analysis, planning, learning, work, and evaluation to model and teach the team how to learn and work independently over time; gradually release team leadership to teams over time; provide learning opportunities for team members and faculty on the collaborative professional learning process; provide learning opportunities for team leaders to learn effective facilitation and learning designs; coach team leaders to become skillful in leading collaborative professional learning; facilitate meetings of team leaders to problem solve and develop new strategies to support team learning and work.	Facilitate team data analysis, planning, learning, work, and evaluation to model and teach the team how to learn and work independently over time; provide learning opportunities for team members and faculty on the collaborative professional learning process; provide learning opportunities for team leaders to learn effective facilitation and learning designs; coach team leaders to become skillful in leading collaborative professional learning; facilitate meetings of team leaders to problem solve and develop new strategies to support team learning and work.	Facilitate team data analysis, planning, learning, work, and evaluation to model and teach the team how to learn and work independently over time; provide learning opportunities for team members and faculty on the collaborative professional learning process; provide learning opportunities for team leaders to learn effective facilitation and learning designs; facilitate meetings of team leaders to problem solve and develop new strategies to support team learning and work.	Facilitate team data analysis, planning, learning, work, and evaluation to model and teach the team how to learn and work independently over time; provide learning opportunities for team members and faculty on the collaborative professional learning process; provide learning opportunities for team leaders to learn effective facilitation and learning designs.	Provide learning opportunities for team members and faculty on the collaborative professional learning process; provide learning opportunities for team leaders to learn effective facilitation and learning designs.	Provide learning opportunities for team members and faculty on the collaborative professional learning process.

TEACHER SUPPORT

5.3: In learning schools, teachers actively participate in multiple learning teams.

Level 1	Level 2	Level 3	Level 4	Level 5	Level 6
Participate in multiple teams, including a grade-level, department, or course-focused learning team, to accomplish educator and student learning goals, whole-school learning team focused on student and educator schoolwide learning goals, or grade-level, content-area, and course teams focused on vertical alignment of curriculum, assessment, and instruction; meet the expectations for full participation as a team member; contribute to the team's learning and work; reflect as a team on individual and team progress toward professional learning goals and student learning goals.	Participate in multiple teams, including a grade-level, department, or course-focused learning team, to accomplish educator and student learning goals, whole-school learning team focused on student and educator schoolwide learning goals or cross grade-level, content-area, and course teams focused on vertical alignment of curriculum, assessment, and instruction; contribute to the team's learning and work; reflect as a team on individual and team progress toward professional learning goals and student learning goals.	Participate in multiple teams, including a grade-level, department, or course-focused learning team, to accomplish educator and student learning goals, whole-school learning team focused on student and educator schoolwide learning goals, or cross grade-level, content-area, and course teams focused on vertical alignment of curriculum, assessment, and instruction.	Participate in a single team, including a grade-level, department, or course-focused learning team, to accomplish educator and student learning goals, whole-school learning team focused on student and educator schoolwide learning goals, or content-area and course teams focused on vertical alignment of curriculum, assessment, and instruction; meet the expectations for full participation as a team member; contribute to the team's learning and work; reflect as a team on individual and team progress toward professional learning goals and student learning goals.	Participate in a single team, including a grade-level, department, or course-focused learning team, to accomplish educator and student learning goals, whole-school learning team focused on student and educator schoolwide learning goals, or content-area and course teams focused on vertical alignment of curriculum, assessment, and instruction; contribute to the team's learning and work; reflect as a team on individual and team progress toward professional learning goals and student learning goals.	Participate in a single team, including a grade-level, department, or course-focused learning team, to accomplish educator and student learning goals.

CLASSROOM IMPLEMENTATION

5.4: In learning schools, teachers implement and reflect on their learning in their classrooms.

Level 1	Level 2	Level 3	Level 4	Level 5	Level 6
Implement learning from collaborative professional learning teams in the classroom; gather data from the classroom to share with the team to assess effectiveness of the intervention; report to team members the effect of interventions on student learning; adapt instruction and classroom curriculum to align with student learning needs and goals; reflect on individual progress toward professional learning goals and student learning goals.	Implement learning from collaborative professional learning teams in the classroom; gather data from the classroom to share with the team to assess effectiveness of the intervention; report to team members the effect of interventions on student learning; adapt instruction and classroom curriculum to align with student learning needs and goals; reflect on individual progress toward professional learning goals and student learning goals.	Implement learning from collaborative professional learning teams in the classroom; adapt instruction and classroom curriculum to align with student learning needs and goals; reflect on individual progress toward professional learning.	Implement learning from collaborative professional learning teams in the classroom; adapt instruction and classroom curriculum to align with student learning needs and goals.	Implement learning from collaborative professional learning teams in the classroom.	

DISTRICT SUPPORT FOR COLLABORATIVE PROFESSIONAL LEARNING

Outcome 6: Learning schools receive support from district leaders who support collaborative professional learning through policy, resources, expectations, professional learning, and ongoing support.

DISTRICT LEADER SUPPORT

6.1: District leaders support learning schools.

Level 1	Level 2	Level 3	Level 4	Level 5	Level 6
Advocate for school board policies, guidance documents, and district structures to support collaborative professional learning and embed collaborative learning teams in both principal and teacher performance standards; communicate the importance of collaborative professional learning to the community; allocate resources to support collaborative professional learning; engage district and school leaders in collaborative professional learning teams; provide professional learning and ongoing support for principals and teacher leaders (coaches) on leading, facilitating, supporting, and monitoring collaborative professional learning teams; develop and support teacher leaders (coaches) to facilitate learning teams; coordinate ongoing cross-school collaboration to share successes and address challenges.	Allocate resources to support collaborative professional learning; engage district and school leaders in collaborative professional learning teams; provide professional learning and ongoing support for principals and teacher leaders (coaches) on leading, facilitating, supporting, and monitoring collaborative professional learning teams; develop and support teacher leaders (coaches) to facilitate learning teams; coordinate ongoing cross-school collaboration to share successes and address challenges.	Allocate resources to support collaborative professional learning; provide professional learning and ongoing support for principals and teacher leaders (coaches) on leading, facilitating, supporting, and monitoring collaborative professional learning teams; develop and support teacher leaders (coaches) to facilitate learning teams; coordinate ongoing cross-school collaboration to share successes and address challenges.	Allocate resources to support collaborative professional learning; provide professional learning and ongoing support for principals and teacher leaders (coaches) on leading, facilitating, supporting, and monitoring collaborative professional learning teams; develop and support teacher leaders (coaches) to facilitate learning teams.	Provide professional learning and ongoing support for principals and teacher leaders (coaches) on leading, facilitating, supporting, and monitoring collaborative professional learning teams, and develop and support teacher leaders (coaches) to facilitate learning teams.	Endorse collaborative professional learning without providing specific support to schools.

Using the Innovation Configuration (IC) maps

The goal of professional development is to improve student learning by enhancing teachers' knowledge and skills. Innovation Configuration (IC) maps can help guide practitioners in developing the means to reach the goal of higher student achievement by providing descriptions of how to implement a practice in a way that will yield results.

The school leadership team can use IC maps in a variety of ways (Roy & Hord, 2004, p. 58):

1. **To provide a clear and descriptive vision of what the standards look like in action.** For example, after reading and discussing the Leadership standard, the school leadership team can analyze the IC maps for the roles of principal, teachers, and the school-based coach to identify what knowledge and skills each needs in order to develop to a high level of implementation of that standard.

2. **To assess implementation of the standards.** The school leadership team can use the IC maps as rubrics to determine the current level of implementation of standards for each role group (i.e. principal, teacher, coach) and compare current practice with the ideal.

3. **To create precise plans and access sufficient resources to implement the standards.** The leadership team determines how current professional learning aligns with the standards and then focuses on a few standards to begin making changes. Reviewing the desired outcomes for each of the chosen standards and determining where on the continuum (level) current practices fall will help the team plan its next steps.

4. **To design professional learning that teaches what the standards look like in practice and how to use the standards.** The school leadership team can use the IC maps to build staff capacity to create more effective professional learning. The levels on the IC maps describe the desired outcome for each standard when it is fully implemented.

5. **To set goals and plan assistance and coaching for colleagues as they implement the standards.** When the team uses IC maps to assess the staff's current level of implementation, members can identify areas of strength and areas for improvement. Team members then can work with faculty to clarify next steps by examining the next level on the way to reaching ideal practice. The professional learning plan would include interventions appropriate to reaching higher levels of implementation.

SCHOOL-BASED STAFF DEVELOPERS

Learning Communities

Staff development that improves the learning of all students organizes adults into learning communities whose goals are aligned with those of the school and district.

DESIRED OUTCOME 1.1: Initiates structures for learning communities that support teacher and student learning.

LEVEL 1	LEVEL 2	LEVEL 3	LEVEL 4	LEVEL 5	LEVEL 6
Provides information about the roles of team members and meeting protocols to ensure effective use of the time for team meetings. Serves as a skilled facilitator for learning teams. Suggests and provides resources to learning teams to assist them in meeting their goals. Attends team meetings to help members stay focused on goals.	Provides information about the roles of team members and meeting protocols to ensure effective use of time provided for team meetings. Suggests and provides resources to learning teams to assist them in meeting their goals. Attends team meetings to help members stay focused on goals.	Provides information about the roles of team members and meeting protocols to ensure effective use of time provided for team meetings. Attends team meetings to help members stay focused on goals.	Attends team meetings to help members stay focused on goals.	Conducts training on the value of and strategies for collaborative professional learning.	

LEARNING COMMUNITIES: SCHOOL-BASED STAFF DEVELOPERS

DESIRED OUTCOME 1.2: Aligns the work of learning communities with school improvement goals.

LEVEL 1	LEVEL 2	LEVEL 3	LEVEL 4	LEVEL 5	LEVEL 6
Supports and develops teachers to serve as skilled facilitators for school and learning team meetings. Provides opportunities for team members to reflect on work done to reach school improvement goals.	Supports teachers in their role as facilitator for school and learning team meetings. Provides opportunities for team members to reflect on work done to reach school improvement goals.	Supports teachers in their role as facilitator for learning team meetings. Meets periodically with team members to reflect on their work to reach school improvement goals.	Meets with teams to be sure they are working to reach school improvement goals.		

DESIRED OUTCOME 1.3: Sustains teacher collaboration during the school day to improve teaching and learning.

LEVEL 1	LEVEL 2	LEVEL 3	LEVEL 4	LEVEL 5	LEVEL 6
Facilitates discussions among learning team members that assess the effectiveness of instruction at all grade levels. Meets regularly with learning teams during the school day to observe and provide feedback about how teams use time in team meetings. Provides opportunities for team members to discuss and identify professional growth needs and opportunities based on student achievement data.	Facilitates discussions among learning team members that assess the effectiveness of instruction at all grade levels. Meets periodically with learning teams during the school day to observe and provide feedback about how teams use time in team meetings. Provides opportunities for team members to discuss and identify professional growth needs and opportunities.	Meets with grade-level leaders to gather information about the effectiveness of instruction. Meets periodically with learning teams during the school day to observe and provide feedback about how teams use time in team meetings. Provides information about professional growth opportunities.	Meets periodically with learning teams during the school day to observe and provide feedback about how teams use time in team meetings. Provides information about professional growth opportunities.		

LEARNING COMMUNITIES: SCHOOL-BASED STAFF DEVELOPERS

DESIRED OUTCOME 1.4: Coordinates work among learning teams to assist members in accomplishing their goals.

LEVEL 1	LEVEL 2	LEVEL 3	LEVEL 4	LEVEL 5	LEVEL 6
Coordinates work across learning teams to be sure content teams, grade-level teams, and vertical teams accomplish their goals and focus on school and district goals. Shares results of work among teams and ensures that team work does not result in duplicated effort. Provides support for staff members as they serve as skilled facilitators during whole-school and learning team meetings.	Coordinates work among learning teams to be sure content teams, grade-level teams, and vertical teams all accomplish their goals and focus on school and district goals. Provides support for staff members as they serve as skilled facilitators during whole-school and learning team meetings.	Meets with learning teams to determine if and how they are accomplishing their goals. Provides support for staff members as they serve as facilitators during learning team meetings.			

DESIRED OUTCOME 1.5: Participates with other coaches in learning communities, some of whose membership extends beyond the school.

LEVEL 1	LEVEL 2	LEVEL 3	LEVEL 4	LEVEL 5	LEVEL 6
Attends regular learning community meetings organized at national, state, regional, and/or district level to identify and solve school challenges as well as learn together with other coaches.	Meets regularly with district learning team. Attends at least one state learning team meeting during the school year.	Meets regularly with district learning team.	Meets informally with coaching colleagues to discuss school challenges.		

SCHOOL-BASED STAFF DEVELOPERS

Leadership

Staff development that improves the learning of all students requires skillful school and district leaders who guide continuous instructional improvement.

DESIRED OUTCOME 2.1: Nurtures a school culture that supports ongoing team-based professional learning.

LEVEL 1	LEVEL 2	LEVEL 3	LEVEL 4	LEVEL 5	LEVEL 6
Recognizes and rewards the accomplishments of teams and improvement efforts. Builds a plan with the staff to support ongoing team learning and improvement. Recognizes the value of team learning and improvement, and discusses improvement activities in staff meetings. Conducts conversations, dialogues, and discussions within the school community until team learning and improvement become a shared goal.	Builds a plan with the staff to support ongoing team learning and improvement. Recognizes the value of team learning and improvement, and discusses improvement activities in staff meetings. Conducts conversations, dialogues, and discussions within the school community until team learning and improvement become a shared goal.	Recognizes the value of team learning, models continuous improvement, and discusses improvement activities in staff meetings. Conducts conversations, dialogues, and discussions within the school community until team learning and improvement become a shared goal.	Conducts conversations, dialogues, and discussions within the school community until team learning and improvement become a shared goal. Communicates that team learning and improvement are essential processes of the school at staff meetings, during evaluations, and with parents and students.	Communicates that team learning and improvement are essential processes of the school at staff meetings.	

LEADERSHIP: SCHOOL-BASED STAFF DEVELOPERS

DESIRED OUTCOME 2.2: Acts as a catalyst to support continuous improvement.

LEVEL 1	LEVEL 2	LEVEL 3	LEVEL 4	LEVEL 5	LEVEL 6
Expects and recognizes team members for their efforts to implement new instructional procedures and share student results. Provides models in which teams review student achievement results, identify high-priority learning goals, and identify new instructional procedures that result in increased learning. Models continuous improvement during staff meetings by discussing current schoolwide results and identifying new processes that result in improvements. Assesses and diagnoses the current school culture to determine which aspects support continuous improvement.	Provides models in which teams review student achievement results, identify high-priority learning goals, and identify new instructional procedures that result in increased learning. Models continuous improvement during staff meetings by discussing current schoolwide results and identifying new processes that result in improvements. Assesses and diagnoses the current school culture to determine which aspects support continuous improvement.	Models continuous improvement during staff meetings by discussing current schoolwide results and identifying new processes that result in improvements. Assesses and diagnoses the current school culture to determine which aspects support continuous improvement.	Uses staff meetings to discuss and identify schoolwide results and to create new procedures that result in improvements. Assesses and diagnoses the current school culture to determine which aspects support continuous improvement.	Assesses and diagnoses the current school culture to determine which aspects support continuous improvement.	

LEADERSHIP: SCHOOL-BASED STAFF DEVELOPERS

DESIRED OUTCOME 2.3: Supports teachers in their development as instructional leaders.

LEVEL 1	LEVEL 2	LEVEL 3	LEVEL 4	LEVEL 5	LEVEL 6
Supports teachers who lead schoolwide committees that make decisions about curriculum, instruction, resources, and professional development. Contributes to the establishment of school guidelines that support these practices. Supports teachers who serve as mentors and master teachers, and supports other instructional coaches.	Supports teachers who serve as mentors and master teachers, and supports other instructional coaches.	Supports teachers as they lead grade-level/content-area meetings.	Identifies leadership opportunities for teachers.		

LEADERSHIP: SCHOOL-BASED STAFF DEVELOPERS

DESIRED OUTCOME 2.4: Participates in professional learning to become a more effective instructional leader.

LEVEL 1	LEVEL 2	LEVEL 3	LEVEL 4	LEVEL 5	LEVEL 6
Participates in facilitated learning teams that problem solve and learn together. Participates in ongoing learning activities that include hands-on experiences focused on authentic problems and supplemented by multiple opportunities for application of the learning. Participates in follow-up, coaching, and feedback. Supports principal in allocating time to explore and practice specific behaviors and strategies and receive feedback on the implementation of new skills.	Participates in ongoing learning activities that include hands-on experiences focused on authentic problems and supplemented by multiple opportunities for application of the learning. Participates in follow-up, coaching, and feedback. Supports principal in allocating time to explore and practice specific behaviors and strategies and receive feedback on the implementation of new skills.	Participates in a series of short-term sessions on instructional leadership and plans to apply new knowledge, skills, and practices during the workday.	Reads articles about instructional leadership.	Does not participate in professional learning experiences related to instructional leadership.	

LEADERSHIP: SCHOOL-BASED STAFF DEVELOPERS

DESIRED OUTCOME 2.5: Engages internal and external stakeholders in planning and implementing high-quality professional learning.

LEVEL 1	LEVEL 2	LEVEL 3	LEVEL 4	LEVEL 5	LEVEL 6
Plans high-quality professional learning with key stakeholders. Monitors implementation of professional development programs to ensure student learning results. Supports principals' expectations for staff implementation of new strategies while creating a system of follow-up to support implementation of new strategies. Works with staff to create a schedule that allows for additional time within the calendar for professional learning. Works with the staff and staff developers to design and implement ongoing professional learning based on assessed student and teacher needs.	Plans high-quality professional learning with key stakeholders. Supports principal's expectations for staff implementation of new strategies while creating a system of follow-up to support implementation of new strategies. Works with staff to create a schedule that allows for additional time within the calendar for professional learning. Works with the staff and staff developers to design and implement ongoing professional learning based on assessed student and teacher needs.	Plans high-quality professional learning with key stakeholders. Works with staff to create a schedule that allows for additional time within the calendar for professional learning. Works with the staff and staff developers to design and implement ongoing professional learning based on assessed student and teacher needs.	Plans high-quality professional learning with key stakeholders. Works with the staff to schedule professional learning activities for designated days in the calendar.		

LEADERSHIP: SCHOOL-BASED STAFF DEVELOPERS

DESIRED OUTCOME 2.6: Articulates the intended results of professional learning on teacher practice and student achievement.

LEVEL 1	LEVEL 2	LEVEL 3	LEVEL 4	LEVEL 5	LEVEL 6
Provides input to principal regarding school-based staff development practices. Creates description of expected changes in instructional practices from school-based staff development. Identifies student results that teachers can expect from changes in their instructional practices.	Creates description of expected changes in instructional practices from school-based staff development. Identifies student results that teachers can expect from changes in their instructional practices.	Creates description of expected changes in instructional practices from school-based staff development.	Describes general outcomes of school-based staff development.	Explains how school-based staff development supports school improvement goals.	

DESIRED OUTCOME 2.7: Advocates for high-quality, school- and team-based professional learning.

LEVEL 1	LEVEL 2	LEVEL 3	LEVEL 4	LEVEL 5	LEVEL 6
Advocates with school board members, community members, community partnerships, colleagues, and central office administrators for high-quality, job-embedded, school-based professional learning.	Advocates with colleagues and central office administrators for high-quality, job-embedded, school-based professional learning.	Advocates with colleagues for high-quality, job-embedded, school-based professional learning.	Supports only professional learning that occurs outside the school.		

LEADERSHIP: SCHOOL-BASED STAFF DEVELOPERS

DESIRED OUTCOME 2.8: Models professional learning for continuous improvement.

LEVEL 1	LEVEL 2	LEVEL 3	LEVEL 4	LEVEL 5	LEVEL 6
Persists with the same learning goals through implementation and mastery. States publicly personal professional learning goals, practices new strategies, and seeks feedback from the staff. Participates in a variety of professional development activities (e.g. reads articles, attends professional conferences, and uses technology to learn about new practices).	States publicly personal professional learning goals, practices new strategies, and seeks feedback from the staff. Participates in a variety of professional development activities (e.g. reads articles, attends professional conferences, and uses technology to learn about new practices).	Participates in a variety of professional development activities (e.g. reads articles, attends professional conferences, and uses technology to learn about new practices).	Participates in only one form of professional development over time focused on a variety of goals at a shallow level.		

SCHOOL-BASED STAFF DEVELOPERS

Resources

Staff development that improves the learning of all students requires resources to support adult learning and collaboration.

DESIRED OUTCOME 3.1: Acts as a resource to support job-embedded professional learning in the school.

LEVEL 1	LEVEL 2	LEVEL 3	LEVEL 4	LEVEL 5	LEVEL 6
Works with principal to allocate resources to create a system of both formal and informal interactions that support professional learning so that staff spends 25% of its time during the work week in learning and collaboration with colleagues.	Works with principal to allocate resources to support school-based staff development that includes regular time within the school day for grade-level, content-area, or whole-staff teams to discuss instruction, curriculum, and assessment.	Works with principal to allocate resources to support time during the workday for the whole staff to reflect on student achievement and identify areas of teacher learning needs.	Makes teachers aware of district professional development calendars, courses, and workshops that require no school resources.		

RESOURCES: SCHOOL-BASED STAFF DEVELOPERS

DESIRED OUTCOME 3.2: Ensures the use of resources to support job-embedded professional learning priorities.

LEVEL 1	LEVEL 2	LEVEL 3	LEVEL 4	LEVEL 5	LEVEL 6
Assists principal in accessing internal and external resources (time and funding) to support the use of internal teacher leaders, coaches, or experts to support teachers in their classrooms. Works with principal to allocate internal and external resources to support master teachers, mentors, and other school- and district-based resource personnel who work with individual teachers and learning teams to apply new or refine existing instructional, curricular, and/or assessment strategies.	Works with principal to allocate internal and external resources (time and funding) to support master teachers, mentors, and other school- and district-based resource personnel who work with teachers and learning teams to use new instructional, curriculum, or assessment strategies.	Assists principal in accessing resources (time and funding) to support the use of external resource personnel or experts to work with teachers in their classrooms to improve instruction.	Assists principal in allocating resources to support teacher attendance at workshops. Gives teachers feedback about their application of new learning in their classrooms.		

RESOURCES: SCHOOL-BASED STAFF DEVELOPERS

DESIRED OUTCOME 3.3: Focuses learning teams' resources on high-priority goals.

LEVEL 1	LEVEL 2	LEVEL 3	LEVEL 4	LEVEL 5	LEVEL 6
Works with staff to focus on a small number of high-priority goals and provides resources to support their accomplishment. Works with principal to ensure resources are not diverted to other competing issues.	Works with principal to identify a small number of goals, but does not encourage principal to dedicate school resources to these goals.	Works with principal, identifies a large number of competing goals which results in a lack of sufficient resources to accomplish goals.	Sets individual goals that are not aligned with school or district goals.		

DESIRED OUTCOME 3.4: Provides external and internal support related to learning priorities.

LEVEL 1	LEVEL 2	LEVEL 3	LEVEL 4	LEVEL 5	LEVEL 6
Works with learning teams to regularly access internal and external expertise to assist with solving instructional problems and improving instructional practice.	Assists teachers in regularly accessing internal and external expertise to assist with solving instructional problems and improving instructional practice.	Assists teachers in accessing internal expertise to assist with solving instructional problems and improving instructional practice.	Limits teacher access to internal and external expertise to assist them with solving instructional problems and improving instructional practice.		

SCHOOL-BASED STAFF DEVELOPERS

Evaluation

Staff development that improves the learning of all students uses multiple sources of information to guide improvement and demonstrate its impact.

DESIRED OUTCOME 5.1: Contributes to the design of formative and summative evaluations of school-based professional learning.

LEVEL 1	LEVEL 2	LEVEL 3	LEVEL 4	LEVEL 5	LEVEL 6
Works collaboratively with principal and staff to conduct formative and summative evaluation to assess the impact of school-based professional learning. Collects beginning-of-year/program and end-of-year/program data about professional learning, including his/her own work as a coach (e.g. learning, implementation, etc.), changes in teacher practice, and student learning to assess impact of professional learning throughout the school year.	Works collaboratively with principal to conduct summative and formative evaluation of professional development to assess the impact of school-based professional learning on teacher practice and student results. Uses results to improve professional development.	Works collaboratively with principal to conduct summative or formative evaluation of professional development to assess the impact of school-based professional learning on teacher practice.	Works collaboratively with principal to conduct summative or formative evaluation of professional development for compliance purposes.	Collects end-of-event satisfaction data about professional development within the school	Collects end-of-year information about professional development, including number of hours provided, teachers participating, programs provided, etc.

EVALUATION: SCHOOL-BASED STAFF DEVELOPERS

DESIRED OUTCOME 5.2: Guides teachers to use data (evidence) from multiple sources to evaluate the impact of professional learning.

LEVEL 1	LEVEL 2	LEVEL 3	LEVEL 4	LEVEL 5	LEVEL 6
Assists teachers and principal to collect and use appropriate data from multiple sources to determine how professional development has impacted teacher practice and student learning. Assists teachers and principal to use data from multiple sources to determine how school culture and organizational structures are changing.	Assists teachers and principal to collect and use appropriate data from two sources to determine how professional development has impacted teacher practice.	Assists teachers and principal to collect and use one appropriate data source to determine how professional development impacts teacher learning.	Collects data from a variety of sources about teacher satisfaction with professional development.	Collects data from a single source about teacher satisfaction with professional development.	

EVALUATION: SCHOOL-BASED STAFF DEVELOPERS

DESIRED OUTCOME 5.3: Facilitates the analysis of classroom and learning team data to determine impact on student achievement, teacher practice, and school culture.

LEVEL 1	LEVEL 2	LEVEL 3	LEVEL 4	LEVEL 5	LEVEL 6
Works collaboratively with principal and teachers to analyze data collected from learning team members about the effectiveness of learning teams. Works collaboratively with principal and teachers to analyze data collected from multiple sources to determine the impact of professional development on teacher practice and student learning. Assists teachers and principal to assess how school culture and organizational structures are changing.	Works collaboratively with principal and teachers to analyze data collected from multiple sources to determine the impact of professional development on teacher practice and student learning. Assists teachers and principal to assess how school culture and organizational structures are changing.	Works collaboratively with principal to analyze data collected from one source to determine the impact of professional development on teacher practice and student learning. Assists principal to assess how school culture and organizational structures are changing.	Assists principal to analyze data from one source to determine how professional development impacts teacher practice and student learning.	Shares analyzed data with principal and teachers about the impact of professional development on teacher practice and student learning.	Shares analyzed data with principal and teachers about the impact of professional development on teacher practice.

SCHOOL-BASED STAFF DEVELOPERS

Design

Staff development that improves the learning of all students uses learning strategies appropriate to the intended goal.

DESIRED OUTCOME 7.1: Designs and facilitates a variety of in-depth, sustained professional learning experiences aligned with the school improvement goals for student achievement.

LEVEL 1	LEVEL 2	LEVEL 3	LEVEL 4	LEVEL 5	LEVEL 6
Designs and facilitates a variety of in-depth, sustained, and collaborative professional learning experiences (e.g. lesson study, peer coaching, examining student work, study groups, writing and scoring common assessments, joint instructional planning, etc.) that align with school improvement goals for student achievement, that work together as a coherent whole, and that place responsibility primarily on participants for their learning. Makes connections between the work of collaborative teams and the larger goal of improving student learning. Designs learning strategies based on clearly stated outcomes for teacher and student learning. Collects and uses data from teacher concern and prior knowledge surveys, classroom observations, informal conversations with teachers, and current schoolwide student data to design professional learning opportunities for deepening content knowledge and refining instructional practices.	Designs and facilitates a variety of in-depth, sustained, and collaborative professional learning experiences (e.g. lesson study, peer coaching, examining student work, study groups, writing and scoring common assessments, joint instructional planning, etc.) that align with school improvement goals for student achievement, that work together as a coherent whole, and that place responsibility primarily on participants for their learning. Makes connections between the work of collaborative teams and the larger goal of improving student learning. Designs learning strategies based on clearly stated outcomes for teacher and student learning.	Designs and facilitates a variety of in-depth, sustained, and collaborative professional learning experiences (e.g. lesson study, peer coaching, examining student work, study groups, writing and scoring common assessments, joint instructional planning, etc.) that align with school improvement goals for student achievement, that work together as a coherent whole, and that place responsibility primarily on participants for their learning. Designs learning strategies based on clearly stated outcomes for teacher and student learning.	Designs and facilitates a variety of in-depth, sustained, and collaborative professional learning experiences (e.g. lesson study, peer coaching, examining student work, study groups, writing and scoring common assessments, joint instructional planning, etc.) that align with school improvement goals for student achievement, that work together as a coherent whole, and that place responsibility primarily on participants for their learning.	Uses a specific professional learning design for most or all professional learning experiences.	

DESIGN: SCHOOL-BASED STAFF DEVELOPERS

DESIRED OUTCOME 7.2: Supports implementation of new and/or refined instructional practices that result from in-depth, sustained professional learning.

LEVEL 1	LEVEL 2	LEVEL 3	LEVEL 4	LEVEL 5	LEVEL 6
Works with principal and teachers to create tools, such as checklists, innovation configuration maps, rubrics, etc., to describe and support implementation of new and/or refined instructional practices. Facilitates daily conversations within and among learning teams about teaching and learning. Sustains conversations over time to examine continuous improvement. Provides concrete examples of successful implementation. Helps teachers access resources to support implementation. Facilitates problem solving to overcome barriers associated with implementation.	Works with principal and teachers to create tools, such as checklists, innovation configuration maps, rubrics, etc., to describe and support implementation of new and/or refined instructional practices. Facilitates daily conversations within and among learning teams about teaching and learning. Provides concrete examples of successful implementation. Helps teachers access resources to support implementation. Facilitates problem solving to overcome barriers associated with implementation.	Works with principal and teachers to create tools, such as checklists, innovation configuration maps, rubrics, etc., to describe and support implementation of new and/or refined instructional practices. Provides concrete examples of successful implementation. Helps teachers access resources to support implementation. Facilitates problem solving to overcome barriers associated with implementation.	Works with principal and teachers to create tools, such as checklists, innovation configuration maps, rubrics, etc., to describe and support implementation of new and/or refined instructional practices. Provides concrete examples of successful implementation.	Works with principal and teachers to create tools, such as checklists, innovation configuration maps, rubrics, etc., to describe and support implementation of new and/or refined instructional practices.	

DESIGN: SCHOOL-BASED STAFF DEVELOPERS

DESIRED OUTCOME 7.3: Provides classroom-based support for implementation of new and/or refined instructional practices.

LEVEL 1	LEVEL 2	LEVEL 3	LEVEL 4	LEVEL 5	LEVEL 6
Selects classroom-based support that aligns with teachers' level of comfort and expertise (e.g. years of experience, current knowledge and skills, etc.). Provides demonstration, co-teaching, and observation and feedback to support implementation of new and refined instructional practices. Designs and supports multiple classroom experiences that deepen understanding and meaning of new concepts and strategies. Engages teachers in conducting peer coaching or walk-throughs to see examples of implementation. Facilitates teachers to problem solve and adapt new strategies to match classroom and individual student learning needs, content, and other circumstances. Seeks teacher feedback to improve coaching skills and practices.	Selects classroom-based support that aligns with teachers' level of comfort and expertise (e.g. years of experience, current knowledge and skills, etc.). Provides demonstration, co-teaching, and observation and feedback to support implementation of new and refined instructional practices. Designs and supports multiple classroom experiences that deepen understanding and meaning of new concepts and strategies. Engages teachers in conducting peer coaching or walk-throughs to see examples of implementation. Facilitates teachers to problem solve and adapt new strategies to match classroom and individual student learning needs, content, and other circumstances.	Provides demonstration, co-teaching, and observation and feedback to support implementation of new and refined instructional practices. Engages teachers in conducting peer coaching or walk-throughs to see examples of implementation. Facilitates teachers to problem solve and adapt new strategies to match classroom and individual student learning needs, content, and other circumstances.	Provides demonstration, co-teaching, and observation and feedback to support implementation of new and refined instructional practices. Facilitates teachers to problem solve and adapt new strategies to match classroom and individual student learning needs, content, and other circumstances.	Leads discussions on how new practices may be implemented. Visits classrooms to observe the implementation of new and/or refined instructional practices. Gives feedback to teachers about their implementation of new and/or refined instructional practices.	Visits classrooms to observe the implementation of new and/or refined practices. Gives feedback to teachers about their implementation of new and/or refined instructional practices.

DESIGN: SCHOOL-BASED STAFF DEVELOPERS

DESIRED OUTCOME 7.4: Engages teachers in reflection to refine and integrate effective classroom practices.

LEVEL 1	LEVEL 2	LEVEL 3	LEVEL 4	LEVEL 5	LEVEL 6
Engages teachers in reflective teaching and learning conversations using a variety of tools. Supports teachers as they reflect on previously taught lessons for the purpose of improving or refining instruction. Leads teachers in the discovery that reflection is a powerful teaching practice.	Engages teachers in reflective teaching and learning conversations using a variety of tools. Supports teachers as they reflect on previously taught lessons for the purpose of improving or refining instruction.	Promotes the use of continuous reflection as a standard practice for improvement. Supports teachers as they reflect on previously taught lessons for the purpose of improving or refining instruction.	Supports teachers as they reflect on previously taught lessons for the purpose of improving or refining instruction.		

DESIGN: SCHOOL-BASED STAFF DEVELOPERS

DESIRED OUTCOME 7.5: Engages teachers using technology for collegial exchange as a component of professional learning when appropriate.

LEVEL 1	LEVEL 2	LEVEL 3	LEVEL 4	LEVEL 5	LEVEL 6
Networks with coaches at the national, state, and/or regional levels to establish electronic collegial relationships among teachers that support professional learning aligned with similar school improvement goals. Makes available the use of appropriate technology for professional learning opportunities (e.g. enrolling in online courses, participating in action research studies, sharing lessons and results with other teachers) that extend beyond the school.	Makes available the use of appropriate technology for professional learning opportunities (e.g. enrolling in online courses, participating in action research studies, sharing lessons and results with other teachers) that extend beyond the school.	Relays information about available opportunities to participate in professional learning opportunities (e.g. enrolling in online courses, networking within the district) supported through technology.	Demonstrates how CD-ROMs and e-mail support professional learning. Demonstrates how to conduct research using the Internet and other electronic resources.	Uses technology as a professional learning management tool and in professional learning presentations (e.g. Excel, PowerPoint).	

SCHOOL-BASED STAFF DEVELOPERS

Collaboration

Staff development that improves the learning of all students provides educators with the knowledge and skills to collaborate.

DESIRED OUTCOME 9.1: Reinforces a school culture characterized by trust.

LEVEL 1	LEVEL 2	LEVEL 3	LEVEL 4	LEVEL 5	LEVEL 6
Puts student interests above staff interests. Keeps his/her word and commitments to staff. Believes in teachers' ability and willingness to be effective teachers. Communicates with staff members with respect and courtesy. Encourages staff to express their points of view with clarity. Takes an interest in the personal and professional well-being of all staff members.	Puts student interests above staff interests. Keeps his/her word and commitments to staff. Believes in teachers' ability and willingness to be effective teachers. Communicates with staff members with respect and courtesy. Takes an interest in the personal and professional well-being of all staff members.	Puts student interests above staff interests. Keeps his/her word and commitments to staff. Believes in teachers' ability and willingness to be effective teachers. Communicates with staff members with respect and courtesy.	Puts student interests above staff interests. Keeps his/her word and commitments to staff. Communicates with staff members with respect and courtesy.	Puts student interests above staff interests. Keeps his/her word and commitments to staff.	Puts staff interests above student interests.

COLLABORATION: SCHOOL-BASED STAFF DEVELOPERS

DESIRED OUTCOME 9.2: Creates structures and processes for collaborative work that promote collegiality and shared responsibility.

LEVEL 1	LEVEL 2	LEVEL 3	LEVEL 4	LEVEL 5	LEVEL 6
Works collaboratively with staff across the school to improve the learning of all students. Works collaboratively with teachers to establish structures (team membership, norms, team leaders, times to meet, etc.) and processes (protocols, norms, reporting mechanisms, etc.) for ongoing learning teams focused on improving instructional practice and achievement of all students. Helps teachers work collaboratively in a variety of different teams (grade-level, department, course, interdisciplinary, whole school, etc.). Supports all teachers to be responsible for success of all students.	Works collaboratively with staff across the school to improve the learning of all students. Works collaboratively with teachers to establish structures (team membership, norms, team leaders, times to meet, etc.) and processes (protocols, norms, reporting mechanisms, etc.) for ongoing learning teams focused on improving instructional practice and achievement of all students. Helps teachers work collaboratively in a variety of different teams (grade-level, department, course, interdisciplinary, whole school, etc.).	Works collaboratively with staff across the school to improve the learning of all students. Works collaboratively with teachers to establish structures (team membership, norms, team leaders, times to meet, etc.) and processes (protocols, norms, reporting mechanisms, etc.) for ongoing learning teams focused on improving instructional practice and achievement of all students.	Works collaboratively with staff across the school to improve the learning of all students.	Works collaboratively with individual teachers to improve student learning within their classrooms.	

COLLABORATION: SCHOOL-BASED STAFF DEVELOPERS

DESIRED OUTCOME 9.3: Provides informal and formal opportunities to learn and apply collaborative skills.

LEVEL 1	LEVEL 2	LEVEL 3	LEVEL 4	LEVEL 5	LEVEL 6
Creates opportunities for teachers to learn from each other about how to improve teaching and learning experiences. Provides resources and materials on effective collaboration skills. Provides opportunities for teachers to practice collaboration skills, including team decision making, stating points of view, inquiring, advocating, listening, paraphrasing, etc. Helps teachers assess the effectiveness of their collaboration skills. Seeks feedback on his/her collaboration skills. Assists teachers to apply trust-building and collaboration skills with students and other adults.	Creates opportunities for teachers to learn from each other about how to improve teaching and learning experiences. Provides opportunities for teachers to practice collaboration skills, including team decision making, stating points of view, inquiring, advocating, listening, paraphrasing, etc. Helps teachers assess the effectiveness of their collaboration skills. Seeks feedback on his/her collaboration skills. Assists teachers to apply trust-building and collaboration skills with students and other adults.	Creates opportunities for teachers to learn from each other about how to improve teaching and learning experiences. Provides resources and materials on effective collaboration skills. Provides opportunities for teachers to practice collaboration skills, including team decision making, stating points of view, inquiring, advocating, listening, paraphrasing, etc. Helps teachers assess the effectiveness of their collaboration skills.	Creates opportunities for teachers to learn from each other about how to improve teaching and learning experiences. Provides resources and materials on effective collaboration skills. Provides opportunities for teachers to practice collaboration skills, including team decision making, stating points of view, inquiring, advocating, listening, paraphrasing, etc.	Creates opportunities for teachers to learn from each other about how to improve teaching and learning experiences. Provides resources and materials on effective collaboration skills.	

COLLABORATION: SCHOOL-BASED STAFF DEVELOPERS

DESIRED OUTCOME 9.4: Models use of effective collaboration skills.

LEVEL 1	LEVEL 2	LEVEL 3	LEVEL 4	LEVEL 5	LEVEL 6
Models collaboration and debriefs interactions to highlight effective collaboration skills. Implements knowledge about group development, decision making, and effective interaction collaboration skills when working with colleagues. Participates as a member in schoolwide committees and other collaborative teams. Alters group process to accommodate various developmental stages of groups he/she is working with. Coaches other teacher leaders on how to use effective collaboration skills in facilitating, leading, and/or working with groups.	Models collaboration and debriefs interactions to highlight effective collaboration skills. Implements knowledge about group development, decision making, and effective interaction collaboration skills when working with colleagues. Participates as a member in schoolwide committees and other collaborative teams. Alters group process to accommodate various developmental stages of groups he/she is working with.	Models collaboration and debriefs interactions to highlight effective collaboration skills. Implements knowledge about group development, decision making, and effective interaction collaboration skills when working with colleagues. Participates as a member in schoolwide committees and other collaborative teams.	Models collaboration and debriefs interactions to highlight effective collaboration skills. Implements knowledge about group development, decision making, and effective interaction collaboration skills when working with colleagues.	Models collaboration skills.	

COLLABORATION: SCHOOL-BASED STAFF DEVELOPERS

DESIRED OUTCOME 9.5: Engages staff in learning and applying effective conflict resolution skills.

LEVEL 1	LEVEL 2	LEVEL 3	LEVEL 4	LEVEL 5	LEVEL 6
Provides experiences for teachers to gain knowledge of ways to resolve conflict. Provides opportunities for teachers to learn strategies for constructive conflict resolution. Provides resources and materials on effective conflict resolution skills. Assists teachers to apply conflict resolution skills. Coaches teachers to mediate or facilitate conflict resolution.	Provides experiences for teachers to gain knowledge of ways to resolve conflict. Provides opportunities for teachers to learn strategies for constructive conflict resolution. Provides resources and materials on effective conflict resolution skills. Assists teachers to apply conflict resolution skills. Mediates or facilitates conflict resolution.	Provides experiences for teachers to gain knowledge of ways to resolve conflict. Provides opportunities for teachers to learn strategies for constructive conflict resolution. Provides resources and materials on effective conflict resolution skills. Assists teachers to apply conflict resolution skills.	Provides experiences for teachers to gain knowledge of ways to resolve conflict. Provides opportunities for teachers to learn strategies for constructive conflict resolution. Provides resources and materials on effective conflict resolution skills.	Provides resources and materials on effective conflict resolution skills.	

DESIRED OUTCOME 9.6: Uses effective conflict resolution skills with staff.

LEVEL 1	LEVEL 2	LEVEL 3	LEVEL 4	LEVEL 5	LEVEL 6
Manages conflicts with colleagues productively. Serves as a role model for staff on how to resolve conflict constructively. Creates opportunities for staff members to share different perspectives in a risk-free forum.	Manages conflicts with colleagues productively. Serves as a role model for staff on how to resolve conflict constructively.	Manages conflicts with colleagues productively.	Invites colleagues to resolve conflicts productively.		

COLLABORATION: SCHOOL-BASED STAFF DEVELOPERS

DESIRED OUTCOME 9.7: Uses technology to facilitate collegial interactions among staff.

LEVEL 1	LEVEL 2	LEVEL 3	LEVEL 4	LEVEL 5	LEVEL 6
Engages teachers in collaborating about teaching and learning through online discussion forums, online courses, wikis, blogs, webinars, etc. Encourages staff to participate in online content-area networks, conduct action research, and share and seek resources electronically. Engages staff in using online decision-making tools. Moderates web-based learning among staff.	Engages teachers in collaborating about teaching and learning through online discussion forums, online courses, wikis, blogs, webinars, etc. Encourages staff to participate in online content-area networks, conduct action research, and share and seek resources electronically. Engages staff in using online decision-making tools.	Engages teachers in collaborating about teaching and learning through online discussion forums, online courses, wikis, blogs, webinars, etc. Encourages staff to participate in online content-area networks, conduct action research, and share and seek resources electronically.	Encourages staff to participate in online content-area networks, conduct action research, and share and seek resources electronically.	Shares web-based interactive resources with staff, including online discussion forums, online courses, webinars, etc.	

COLLABORATION: SCHOOL-BASED STAFF DEVELOPERS

DESIRED OUTCOME 9.8: Uses technology to collaborate with teachers, principal, and other coaches.

LEVEL 1	LEVEL 2	LEVEL 3	LEVEL 4	LEVEL 5	LEVEL 6
Communicates effectively with teachers, principal, and other coaches via e-mail. Researches, critiques, and shares web-based interactive resources with staff, principal, and other coaches, including online discussion forums, online courses, webinars, etc. Collaborates with other coaches about teaching and learning through online discussion forums, online courses, wikis, blogs, webinars, etc. Participates in an online community.	Communicates effectively with teachers, principal, and other coaches via e-mail. Researches, critiques, and shares web-based interactive resources with staff, principal, and other coaches, including online discussion forums, online courses, webinars, etc. Collaborates with other coaches about teaching and learning through online discussion forums, online courses, wikis, blogs, webinars, etc.	Communicates effectively with teachers, principal, and other coaches via e-mail. Researches, critiques, and shares web-based interactive resources with staff and principal, including online discussion forums, online courses, webinars, etc. Collaborates with other coaches about teaching and learning through online discussion forums, online courses, wikis, blogs, webinars, etc.	Communicates effectively with teachers, principal, and other coaches via e-mail. Collaborates with other coaches about teaching and learning through online discussion forums, online courses, wikis, blogs, webinars, etc.	Communicates effectively with teachers, principal, and other coaches via e-mail.	

SCHOOL-BASED STAFF DEVELOPERS

Quality Teaching

Staff development that improves the learning of all students deepens educators' content knowledge, provides them with research-based instructional strategies to assist students in meeting rigorous academic standards, and prepares them to use various types of classroom assessments appropriately.

DESIRED OUTCOME 11.1: Advances staff's deep understanding and use of content knowledge and research-based instructional strategies to help students meet rigorous academic standards.

LEVEL 1	LEVEL 2	LEVEL 3	LEVEL 4	LEVEL 5	LEVEL 6
Facilitates professional development to develop staff's deep understanding of content knowledge and research-based instructional strategies. Demonstrates the use of research-based instructional strategies in classrooms. Integrates research-based instructional strategies into professional development he/she provides to staff. Participates in professional development to deepen his/her own content knowledge and research-based instructional strategies. Provides classroom-based support to teachers in using content knowledge and research-based instructional strategies. Facilitates teachers' planning of discipline-specific and interdisciplinary units that focus on major content-area concepts.	Facilitates professional development to develop staff's deep understanding of content knowledge and research-based instructional strategies. Demonstrates the use of research-based instructional strategies in classrooms. Provides classroom-based support to teachers in using content knowledge and research-based instructional strategies. Facilitates teachers' planning of discipline-specific and interdisciplinary units that focus on major content-area concepts.	Facilitates professional development to develop staff's deep understanding of content knowledge and research-based instructional strategies. Demonstrates the use of research-based instructional strategies in classrooms. Provides classroom-based support to teachers in using content knowledge and research-based instructional strategies.	Facilitates professional development to develop staff's deep understanding of content knowledge and research-based instructional strategies.	Demonstrates superficial knowledge of content knowledge and research-based instructional knowledge.	Assumes teachers have deep content knowledge and use research-based instructional strategies.

QUALITY TEACHING: SCHOOL-BASED STAFF DEVELOPERS

DESIRED OUTCOME 11.2: Advances staff understanding and use of various strategies to assess student progress toward established goals and to improve teaching practice.

LEVEL 1	LEVEL 2	LEVEL 3	LEVEL 4	LEVEL 5	LEVEL 6
Facilitates professional development on the use of a variety of classroom-based assessments. Demonstrates the use and analysis of various assessment strategies in classrooms. Promotes the use of various classroom, grade-level, department, and schoolwide assessment strategies in individual, small-group, and large-group meetings with staff. Uses various assessment strategies in professional development he/she provides to staff. Provides classroom-based support to teachers in using various assessment strategies. Facilitates teachers' development, use, and analysis of various assessment strategies and common assessments to plan instruction. Engages staff in conversations about the value of various assessment strategies as a means to measure student progress. Notes in classroom observations teachers' use of various assessment strategies.	Facilitates professional development on the use of a variety of classroom-based assessments. Demonstrates the use and analysis of various assessment strategies in classrooms. Promotes the use of various classroom, grade-level, department, and schoolwide assessment strategies in individual, small-group, and large-group meetings with staff. Facilitates teachers' development, use, and analysis of various assessment strategies and common assessments to plan instruction. Engages staff in conversations about the value of various assessment strategies as a means to measure student progress. Notes in classroom observations teachers' use of various assessment strategies.	Facilitates professional development on the use of a variety of classroom-based assessments. Promotes the use of various classroom, grade-level, department, and schoolwide assessment strategies in individual, small-group, and large-group meetings with staff. Engages staff in conversations about the value of various assessment strategies as a means to measure student progress. Notes in classroom observations teachers' use of various assessment strategies.	Facilitates professional development on the development and use of a variety of classroom-based assessments.	Explains the value of various classroom, grade-level, department, or schoolwide assessments.	

QUALITY TEACHING: SCHOOL-BASED STAFF DEVELOPERS

DESIRED OUTCOME 11.3: Assures that time available for professional learning and collaboration is used to enhance quality teaching and student learning.

LEVEL 1	LEVEL 2	LEVEL 3	LEVEL 4	LEVEL 5	LEVEL 6
Establishes agendas for team and schoolwide meetings that focus on quality teaching and student learning. Facilitates team and schoolwide meetings focused on enhancing quality teaching and student learning. Focuses one-on-one meetings with teachers on issues of quality teaching and student learning. Challenges colleagues who redirect the agenda to personal or noninstructional topics. Assists the principal in determining appropriate uses of planning and professional development time so that it is spent focusing on quality teaching and student learning.	Establishes agendas for team and schoolwide meetings that focus on quality teaching and student learning. Facilitates team and schoolwide meetings focused on enhancing quality teaching and student learning. Focuses one-on-one meetings with teachers on issues of quality teaching and student learning. Assists the principal in determining appropriate uses of planning and professional development time so that it is spent focusing on quality teaching and student learning.	Establishes agendas for team and schoolwide meetings that focus on quality teaching and student learning. Facilitates team and schoolwide meetings focused on enhancing quality teaching and student learning. Assists the principal in determining appropriate uses of planning and professional development time so that it is spent focusing on quality teaching and student learning.	Establishes agendas for team and schoolwide meetings that focus on quality teaching and student learning. Assists the principal in determining appropriate uses of planning and professional development time so that it is spent focusing on quality teaching and student learning.	Spends the majority of time in one-on-one, team, or schoolwide meetings focusing on noninstructional topics.	

QUALITY TEACHING: SCHOOL-BASED STAFF DEVELOPERS

DESIRED OUTCOME 11.4: Cultivates a culture that supports innovation and continuous improvement of teaching.

LEVEL 1	LEVEL 2	LEVEL 3	LEVEL 4	LEVEL 5	LEVEL 6
Establishes with colleagues a relationship of trust, risk taking, and support that fosters innovation and change. Models innovation in his/her own work. Celebrates change with colleagues. Helps colleagues learn from mistakes. Acknowledges his/her own learning challenges with implementing innovation and learning from mistakes. Challenges colleagues who are comfortable with the status quo by using data and offering support. Engages teachers in ongoing conversations about what is working and what is not. Supports teachers in asking challenging questions. Encourages colleagues to learn about and share innovative instructional and assessment strategies.	Establishes with colleagues a relationship of trust, risk taking, and support that fosters innovation and change. Celebrates change with colleagues. Helps colleagues learn from mistakes. Challenges colleagues who are comfortable with the status quo by using data and offering support. Engages teachers in ongoing conversations about what is working and what is not. Supports teachers in asking challenging questions. Encourages colleagues to learn about and share innovative instructional and assessment strategies.	Establishes with colleagues a relationship of trust, risk taking, and support that fosters innovation and change. Engages teachers in ongoing conversations about what is working and what is not. Encourages colleagues to learn about and share innovative instructional and assessment strategies.	Engages teachers in ongoing conversations about what is working and what is not. Supports teachers in asking challenging questions. Encourages colleagues to learn about innovative instructional and assessment strategies.	Encourages colleagues to learn about innovative instructional and assessment strategies.	Accepts that not all teachers will continue to improve their practice or their results. Is comfortable with the status quo.

References

Allen, D. & Blythe, T. (2004). *The facilitator's book of questions: Tools for looking together at student and teacher work.* New York: Teachers College Press.

Barth, R. (1997, March 5). The leader as learner. *Education Week.*

Brookover, W.B. & Lezotte, L. (1982). *Creating effective schools.* Holmes Beach, FL: Learning Publications.

Camburn, E.M. & Han, S.W. (2008). Investigating connections between distributed leadership and instructional change. In A. Harris (Ed.), *Distributed leadership: Different perspectives.* New York: Springer.

Conzemius, A. & O'Neill, J. (2002). *The handbook for SMART school teams.* Bloomington, IN: Solution Tree.

Covey, S.R. (2010, April 20). Our children and the crisis in education. *The Huffington Post.* Available online at www.huffingtonpost.com/stephen-r-covey/our-children-and-the-cris_b_545034.html.

Croft, A., Coggshall, J., Dolan, M., Powers, E. (with Killion, J.) (2010, April). Job-embedded professional development: What it is, who is responsible, and how to get it done well. *Issue Brief.* Washington, DC: National Comprehensive Center for Teacher Quality, Mid-Atlantic Comprehensive Center, & NSDC.

Darling-Hammond, L., Wei, R.C., Andree, A., Richardson, N., & Orphanos, S. (2009, February). *Professional learning in the learning profession: A status report on teacher development in the United States and abroad.* Oxford, OH: NSDC.

Dean, C., Galvin, M., & Parsley, D. (2005). *Noteworthy perspectives: Success in sight.* Denver, CO: Midcontinent Research for Education and Learning.

Delehant, A., with von Frank, V. (2007). *Making meetings work: How to get started, get going, and get it done.* Thousand Oaks, CA: Corwin Press with NSDC.

Desimone, L. (2009). Improving impact studies of teachers' professional development: Toward better conceptualizations and measures. *Educational Researcher, 38*(3), 181-199.

Donaldson, G.A., Jr. (2006). *Cultivating leadership in schools: Connecting people, purpose, and practice* (pp. 3-4). New York: Teachers College Press.

DuFour, R. (2004, May). What is a professional learning community? *Educational Leadership, 61*(8), 6-11.

DuFour, R. (2002, May). The learning-centered principal. *Educational Leadership, 59*(8), 12-15.

Duke, D.L. (1982, October). What

can principals do? Leadership functions and instructional effectiveness. *NASSP Bulletin, 66*(456), 1-12.

Easton, L.B. (2009). *Protocols for professional learning.* Alexandria, VA: ASCD.

Easton, L.B. (2008). *Powerful designs for professional learning* (2nd ed.). Oxford, OH: NSDC.

Elmore, R. (2002, May). Hard questions about practice. *Educational Leadership, 59*(8), 22-25.

Elmore, R. (2000, Winter). *Building a new structure for new school leadership.* Washington, DC: The Albert Shanker Institute.

Fisher, D. & Frey, N. (2004). *Improving adolescent literacy: Strategies at work.* Columbus, OH: Pearson Education.

Fullan, M. (2004). *Leadership & sustainability: System thinkers in action.* Thousand Oaks, CA: Corwin Press.

Fullan, M. (1991). *The meaning of educational change* (2nd ed.). Toronto, Ontario, Canada: OISE Press.

Guskey, T. (2001). *Evaluating professional development.* Thousand Oaks, CA: Corwin Press.

Hall, G. & Hord, S. (2001). *Implementing change: Patterns, principles, and potholes.* Boston: Allyn & Bacon.

Heifetz, R.A. & Laurie, D.L. (1997). The work of leadership. *Harvard Business Review, 75*(1), 124-134.

Hirsh, S. (2009, Fall). A new definition. *JSD, 30*(4), 10-16.

Hirsh, S. (2007, Summer). *White paper.* Unpublished manuscript.

Hord, S., Rutherford, W., Huling-Austin, L., & Hall, G. (1998). *Taking charge of change.* Austin, TX: SEDL.

Iowa Department of Education. (2009). *Iowa professional development model technical guide.* Des Moines, IA: Author.

Jolly, A. (2008). *Team to teach: A facilitator's guide to professional learning teams.* Oxford, OH: NSDC.

Joyce, B. & Showers, B. (2002). *Student achievement through staff development* (3rd ed.). Alexandria, VA: ASCD.

Killion, J. (2008). *Assessing impact: Evaluating staff development* (2nd ed.). Thousand Oaks, CA: Corwin Press & NSDC.

Killion, J. (2003, Fall). 8 smooth steps. *JSD, 24*(4), 14-26.

Killion, J. (2002). *What works in the high school: Results-based staff development.* Oxford, OH: NSDC & NEA.

Killion, J. & Harrison, C. (2006). *Taking the lead: New roles for teachers and school-based coaches.* Oxford, OH: NSDC.

Killion, J. & Roy, P. (2009). *Becoming a learning school.* Oxford, OH: NSDC.

Kouzes, J. & Posner, B. (2008). *The leadership challenge* (4th ed.). San Francisco: Jossey-Bass.

Kroeze, D.J. (1984). Effective principals as instructional leaders: New directions for research. *Administrator's Notebook, 30*(9), 1-4.

Lambert, L. (2003). *Leadership capacity for lasting school improvement.* Alexandria, VA: ASCD.

Leithwood, K., Aitken, R., & Jantzi, D. (2006). *Making schools smarter: Leading with evidence.* Thousand Oaks, CA: Corwin Press.

Levine, D.U. & Lezotte, L.W. (1990). *Unusually effective schools: A review and analysis of research and practice.* Madison, WI: National Center for Effective Schools Research and Development.

Marzano, R.J. (2003). *What works in schools: Translating research into action.* Alexandria, VA: ASCD.

Marzano, R.J., Waters, T., & McNulty, B. (2005). *School leadership that works: From research to results.* Alexandria, VA: ASCD.

McKeever, B. & The California School Leadership Academy. (2003). *Nine lessons of successful school leadership teams.* San Francisco: WestEd.

McLaughlin, M. & Talbert, T. (2006).

Building school-based teacher learning communities. New York: Teachers College Press.

Miller, W.C. & Vruggink, E. (1983, March). Needed: A building-level instructional leader. *The Clearing House, 56*(7), pp. 321-323.

Mortimore, P., Sammons, P., Stoll, L., Lewis, D., & Ecob, R. (1988). *School matters: The junior years.* Somerset: Open Books.

Muir, M. (2006, April). *Research brief: Leadership teams.* Waterville, ME: Maine Center for Meaningful Engaged Learning. Available at www.principalspartnership.com/leadershipteams. pdf.

Murphy, J. (1992). *The landscape of leadership preparation: Reframing the education of school administrators.* Thousand Oaks, CA: Corwin Press.

National Center for Education Statistics. (2005, August). Characteristics of public school teachers' professional development activities: 1999-2000. *Issue Brief.* Washington, DC: U.S. Department of Education.

National Staff Development Council. (2001). *NSDC's standards for staff development.* Oxford, OH: Author.

Pont, B., Nusche, D., & Hopkins, D. (2008). *Improving school leadership: Case studies on system leadership.* Paris, France: Organisation for Economic Co-operation and Development.

Roy, P. & Hord, S. (2004, Spring). Innovation Configurations chart a measured course toward change. *JSD, 25*(2), 54-58.

Roy, P. & Hord, S. (2003). *Moving NSDC's staff development standards into practice: Innovation Configurations.* Oxford, OH: NSDC & SEDL.

Senge, P. (1990). *The fifth discipline: The art & practice of the learning organization.* New York: Currency Doubleday.

Sergiovanni, T. (1992). *Rethinking leadership: A collection of articles.* Thousand Oaks, CA: Corwin Press.

Silins, H. & Mulford, W. (2002). Schools as learning organisations: The case for system, teacher and student learning. *Journal of Educational Administration, 40*(5), 425-446.

Sparks, D. (2004, November). Principals possess a vision of quality professional learning. *Results,* p. 2.

Sparks, D. (1999, Spring). Overview. *Journal of Staff Development, 20*(2), 4.

Stronge, J.H. (1988). A position in transition? *Principal, 67*(5), 32-33.

Yoon, K., Duncan, T., Lee, S., Scarloss, B., & Shapley, K. (2007). *Reviewing the evidence on how teacher professional development affects student achievement* (Issues & Answers Report, REL 2007-No. 033). Washington, DC: U.S. Department of Education.

About the authors

Linda Munger is a senior consultant for the National Staff Development Council. As a national education consultant, her work focuses on facilitating, supporting, and evaluating professional development for schools, districts, regional agencies, and state departments. She has worked with grade-level and department teams, school leadership teams, and district and state advisory councils and task forces in developing comprehensive professional development and evaluation. She received NSDC's best nondissertation award in 2001. She assisted Joellen Killion in developing the *Training Manual for Assessing Impact: Evaluating Staff Development* (NSDC, 2003). She has published articles related to her work and written numerous evaluation reports on the impact of professional development. Munger previously was a classroom teacher and adjunct professor. She lives in Iowa with her husband and has two grown sons.

Valerie von Frank has written extensively about education over several decades as a daily newspaper reporter in multiple states covering public schools and, over the last decade, for NSDC publications, including *JSD, Tools for Schools, The Learning System, The Learning Principal,* and *T3.* She is a former editor of *JSD,* worked as a daily newspaper editor, served as communications director in an urban public school district, and was communications director for a Michigan nonprofit school reform organization. She is co-author with Ann Delehant of *Making Meetings Work: How to Get Started, Get Going, and Get It Done* (Corwin Press, 2007). She is currently NSDC's book editor and a freelance writer and editor. She and her husband live in Michigan and have two daughters in public schools.